forward**poetry**

Whispering Words

A Collection Of Poetry

Edited By *Donna Samworth*

First published in Great Britain in 2015 by:
Forward Poetry
Remus House
Coltsfoot Drive
Peterborough
PE2 9BF

Telephone: 01733 890099
Website: www.forwardpoetry.co.uk

Foreword

Here at Forward Poetry our aim has always been to provide a bridge to publication for unknown poets and allow their work to reach a wider audience. We believe that poetry should not be exclusive or elitist but available to be accessed and appreciated by all.

We hope you will agree that our latest collection with its combination of traditional and modern verse is one that everyone can enjoy. Whether you prefer humorous rhymes or poignant odes there is something inside these pages that will suit every reader's taste.

We are very proud to present this anthology and we are sure it will provide entertainment and inspiration for years to come.

Contents

The Poems

A Poem Inspired By Sylvia Plath's 'Mirror'

'Mirror, mirror on the wall, who is the fairest of them all?'
My love, for far too long I have swallowed sore sights
Just as it is, unmisted by love or dislike
Yet you appear to be agitated by that?
I have witnessed your tears, observed your cracks

My love, your adoration for yourself is somewhat unrequited
By self-absorption you have been blinded
Once a flourishing splendour, now wilting hope
Contemplating at the curtain rail, your hands bear a segment of disregarded rope.

Is it because you long for your youth?
Or the attention, the affection, mutations of the truth?
Now look at yourself, what is there to see?
An individual, deceived out of simplicity
'By who?' Yourself. And those oblivious of deception's impending toxicity

An abundance of lies has drowned your eyes
From your hands, the disregarded rope is pried
You retire onto your knees, and to myself you plead,
'End my torment. I have matured into one of life's weeds.'

Emma Myring

1

Speaking In Southern Cemetery

Having spoken little of twenty-four years,
there are a few things that could've been undone,
now this absence renders my dumb tongue,
restraints evaporated with dead bodies
we hide underground. Unsightly images uprooted.
It is here I retrace these fragile limits -
depository of still bodies,
ground overgrown, slicked black pathways
like a lost clandestine, encased in the moon's light
a clarity appears. Not this light-bulb illumination
but the smell of a man I once knew.

Charmain Leung

We Share The Glory

They pushed me on the pedestal,
Believing I could never fall.
Do they not know I, too, am flawed?
They want to fly, whilst I struggle to crawl.

They begged me for the sapphire sky,
And the gold past the rainbow high
They weep of joy whilst I bitterly cry
At the lengths I go for these people of mine.

And then when the demons of war
Knock on the Empire's door,
I try to remind them I was always with flaw
But they scream and call for my fall.

We share all the glory,
But only I take the blame.

Dray Raphael Agha

A Duchess

You'd get to the station
One bright early day
With notebook and pencil
In April or May
And there on the platform
Was your special place
To wait for an express
Coming rushing at pace
Perhaps an old Black Five
With wagons in tow
And rusty old tanks
On a local that's slow.
Then out of the distance
Comes dashing at speed
A mighty Pacific
With plenty of steam.
It could be a Duchess
Or Princess that's late
And trying to pick up
Some time at a rate
It rushes right past you
And whistles galore
A sight that is history
And gone now for sure.

Roy T Gough

Just Revealing

Just making a space to find a place to put my words in,
testing the ground that's all around it's just amazing,
what goes on everywhere I put my face in,
I see the sky down below I must be dreaming,
or am I feeling the facts of life that's just revealing?

Vincent Rees

Sunshine

For every day there is a new dawn,
Like a magnet I feel drawn,
Feeling the warmth upon my skin,
I feel alive, I tingle within,
The illumination is all around,
I smile, the joy I found.

As the light fades away,
I wait for you to have your say,
Like a ray of sunshine, you are to me,
Giving me joy, I smile you see,
My dear friend, I want you to know,
You have touched my heart, it now glows.

Like the sun you are far away,
But I have faith that we will meet some day,
Even now I still feel blessed,
To feel your words, I am caressed,
Keep on shining my dear friend,
For you light up my world and that's not the end.

Jo Benson

Only For You

Life without love is life without meaning
A body without a soul is an insignificant being
A heart that does not beat is not heard by anyone
A mind that does not reason is useless to everyone
Life is valued by living; I live mine for you completely
Dreams are for dreaming, I dream only about you
Heart is for beating, mine beats just for you
And the mind is for thinking, I think only of you
I think about you every morning and dream about you every night
I love you more than life itself so I make this promise to myself
To be with you till our last breath, even as we part for death.

Suki Kaur Dhaliwal

Waste Nor Want

Oh dear a waste,
This sort or that sort,
An idle thought or deed,
Or worship of a false kind,
A better use is there for sure,
Our best is only best
When best like truth it is,
To think no wrong or heed no wrong,
To use again all good there is,
No waste in that of sense that is,
What's good for one, is good for another,
Pollution round about always,
Protect against, as best one can,
To know the better, though by example good,
Will stand in stead of all the rest,
Then gain a just reward.

Rachel Taylor

The Fall Of Icarus . . .

And all around the world keeps turning
While his life flow drips – it's ebbing
With rapid breaths, rasping
Heart beat's pulsing

And all around the sun keeps shining
Keeping time with daylight moving
Slowly around a coastline smoothing
To soften pictures of sail boats sailing

And as if his life it had no meaning
With despair his slow departing
A whirlpool, slowly swallowing
His demise – a crash-landing . . .

Estelle Blackman

Let The Burn

Let the burn cinder your heart,
Spreading like wildfire through your veins.
Crushing waves take breath and dreams,
Desolation is your entirety.

Let the sun be a blackened hole,
Shadowing horizons to bleak contour.
The crows fly and crickets chirp,
Carry on blindly – he has come for me.

Let the sorrow eat your soul,
Devouring whispers so silent and still.
Inside is a chaos hellish and raw;
Don't swallow it down, blink the frosted glass.

Let your eyes be puddled sloops,
The mast at sea sways heavy and punched.
Pull rope, strip skin, but stand up tall;
You're going home through storm and teeth.

Jemma Jackson

Duty Disillusioned

We got sent to die.
In fields of distant France,
Where bodies of the innocent lie,
And where hope stood no chance.

The order came from above.
Government decree, with diplomacy,
Commit that ultimate labour of love
To Kill, and to Die, without mercy.

So we went to war.
Engaged in the bloody crusade,
To King and country we swore,
Weren't we so mightily brave?

For the sky was weeping bullets,
The sea was oozing blood,
The sun had fled the darkness,
Oh where, oh where was love?

Love had long deserted us.
Death left us hollow and gaunt,
Conscious no longer fussed,
The nightmares came to haunt.

And we the glorious heroes,
Romanticised for Nation's pride,
Saluted the poppies in rows,
Yet knowing the truth we lied.

We hid behind the lie.
Ignoring the power play and greed,
Never asking why
But for your freedom we bleed.

Heather Price

The Cliff

You can gape for various miles,
You can find your flourishing heart.
Although the fall may be an enduring way down,
However, the view is still an art.

How lines structure the cracks of the cliff,
Your hands suddenly flow to flourish the scenes.
This scene is so wondrous that you catch the sun,
Although when open-handed nothing is there as it seems.

Hearts have been found but are beating tremendously,
As you close your eyelids swiftly in fear.
You picture the scene, which is now very dull.
You then unbolt your eyes gently, everything is clear.

The view, the landscape,
The minuscule detail, which lies upon the nature.
Let us build bonfires to fill the emptiness of humans,
Let us never be conquered by the fear that we see.

Murdered by fear, I wait.
I wait for the movement of life.
But the movement I see,
Is my heart beating with braveness as I stand on this cliff.

I remember the blankets of fields that lied outside of my house,
I remember the ocean of blue that lay on the sky.
I remember the soft sweet voice that I spoke to others,
But all I know now, is this murdering cliff.

Amelia Rose Weaver

My Mental Illness

Walked miles, around the different pubs,
Thinking of being followed.
Carried a knife, in order to retaliate
The threats, that I would contemplate.

People in black leather jackets
Were harmful, as I thought.
I'll rip the next one that I see.
Off the person, that means harm to me.

I get harmful messages from newspapers.
So refuse to read them I would
Messages from the television
Were both harmful and good.

I could talk to the pigeons
From the top, of high tower blocks
For me the rest of the world, was bugged.
Even the public telephone box.

My own house, was bugged I thought
So I cut the earth wires, without being caught
The dolls in the house, were watching me
With felt pen, I blacked their eyes, 'til they couldn't see.

Different colour cars and number plates
Carried messages, both of love and hate.
Everyone was against me, friends and foe alike.
There's nothing wrong with me, thinks I
It's everybody else.

Into hospital, you must go
For a long-awaited cure.
For another three months or so.
Remained, sectioned and secure.

Edward C Massey

The Sad Little Internet Girl

The school bell rings,
It's time to get out of this hell.
Back to home,
Back to the place where she can crack this shell.

But there's one thing there
Destroying her soul
Not with weapons or firearms
But instead with a camera, touch-screen and social control.

Open up the front door
Run up the stairs
And adorn the disguise
Patch yourself up and do some little repairs.

Thick eyeliner and photo booth effects
Nail polish and editing checks.
Rapunzel-length hair
But none of it's real; none of it's fair.

Not the bright-eyed smiles
Or the model-like pouts
Behind the exterior
There is a sadness and a doubt.

Instagram likes are killing her.
Facebook statuses tearing her apart.
Tweets are carnage to the delicate little mind.
Of the girl behind the social media art.

Fake smiles are a rife though
Happy statuses always set
'I love my best one' is a common place phrase
As she takes a picture with the girl she only just met.

The counterfeit personality however,
Is killing her inside
It was a short process for our girl though
Married to the site now, a social networking bride.

Nobody knows though
Not even the people she holds on high regard.
They all think she's okay,
But Facebook's left its mark on her, now she's scarred.

But she's done such a good job though,
Nobody suspects a thing.

Despite the heavy burden she wears
Like a necklace or a ring.

But now it's time to go back now
Hold up the camera in a flattering angle
Press the shutter
But more feelings will be mangled.

But hush little baby,
Don't say a word.
It's all okay now
You've managed to fool the world.

Rachel Vernon

Stars

Shackled to the stars
Without sight and sound,
Suffering infinity behind bars,
Gravity has got me bound.

Blinded by never-ending light,
Exploding my every sense,
Beauty insufferably bright,
My mind is prone and tense.

Suspended to the stars,
Gravity is my terrifying friend,
The whirlwind of life seems so far,
Cascading me to the end.

Kimberly Davidson

Swimmer

Long before you paddled in Calabash Bay
I was lost. When we first caught sight of you
swimming in your mother's inner sea,
currents, that nurtured embryonic growth,
of blood through heart, limbs, brain and mouth called me
further out than I had ever been.

And then the birth. Oh my boy, the surge
the gasp, the pain, the wrench;

The love that many waters cannot quench
flowed through me as a flood.

That resistless tide deluged my fallow earth
before the clutch and drag of Caribbean surf.

What selfish strength I had could not gainsay
the power that other lives possessed to move me.

Concern for helpless kids, their sinking lives
pulled down by accident of colour, class and lies -
wrecking them on ragged rocks – forced from me tears,
washed me with passion, woke me from sleep
to steer them out of ruin and harm:

What option but to act at love's demand?

And so to run, to save. Oh my boy, the surge
the gasp, the pain, the wrench;
The love that many waters cannot quench.

Laurence Cooper

So Far But So Near

The warmth of the blazing sun
Inspires the hopeful life on Earth.
Its light shines through Heaven
And a million of hearth.
Without it there is no day, night or year,
Wonder how,
It's so far but so near.
The blue sky above the sea,
Is a home for many stars and galaxy.
The birds fly across freely,
The puffy clouds glide gleely,
When I stand near the evening shore,
I see the horizon that makes me glow.
Wonder how,
It's so far but so near.
When I see these beautiful things,
These inevitable natural happenings,
I think of you inadvertently.
Wonder how,
You are so far but so near.

Annapurna Bhattacharya

Freedom

Bognor is the place to be,
Where every visitor feels completely free.
There's time to visit friends and places,
Look in on the theatre, museum's cases.
Market and hobby shops,
Outside flowering tubs.
Clowns come to visit every year
All dressed up in colourful gear.
Parks with slides, swings and climbers
Café's still open, full of diners
There are people who come to jump off the pier
Some dressed up to show no fear.
Evenings are warm, street lights a-glowing,
Time to take rest, gentle breeze a-blowing.
Children asleep, all cosy and warm
Ready to start another day as norm.

Jean Smith

Financial Woes

There was once a financial crash,
It was viral like a rash;
Bonds, shares and stocks,
Went through the floor;
Ruined people; broke and poor.

Rich people reduced to beggars
They were broken into bits,
The world economy crashes
Under the poverty lashes.

Look at the poor
Formerly rich, now begging
At the door
So we can cry with poverty songs.

Finally the rich had gone
Financial products were done
Wealth was washed away
Hello! Poor and begging day.

Christopher Gillham

A Place For Joy

There's a little town in Oxfordshire
That sets my heart aglow
With a funny mixture of buildings
All standing row by row
Some of them are ancient
And some are all brand new
I look at them in wonder
Will the people like them too?
I know that the trees and shrubs
That the developers have grown
Will make the town look nice
And deride the old folks moan
For myself I live in a bungalow
On the outskirts of the town
All in a pretty little haven
Of gardens all home grown
And so I view the old and new
With a warmth and joyous feeling
And with an open-hearted view
Whilst through my heart it's stealing.
This happy town of Bicester
With buildings to please the guest
Will stay my happy hometown
Till my bones are laid to rest.

Royston E Herbert

You're Like A Little Ray Of Sunshine

You have got a great personality
Around you I'm always happy
If only you could see
How you bring the best out of me

You're like a little ray of sunshine
That brightens up my day
You're like a little ray of sunshine
That dries my tears away
You're like a little ray of sunshine
That I love more each day
You're like a little ray of sunshine
That I miss when you're away

You are so gentle and kind
You're always on my mind
You make my darkest days so bright
It's you I want to kiss each night

You're like a little ray of sunshine
That brightens up my day
You're like a little ray of sunshine
That dries my tears away
You're like a little ray of sunshine
That I love more than I can say
In my heart you'll always stay

You're like an angel from up above
Together we go like a hand in a glove
Your love shines like the feathers of a dove
You gave me your unconditional love

Michael McNulty

Snapshots

I wipe the smear of blood from her face, see
her smile set in black and white, paper thin,
worn by his care, the touch of hands that she
remembers as she sits waiting for him.

Perhaps she smiles not knowing that he's dead,
lying here half buried in the mud. Maybe
in a week or two she'll hear the knock, read
the words: duty, honour, pride. Then we'll see

a tear drop, quickly wiped away. Pity
I think, then let the photo fall and pluck
instead a button from his coat, a trophy,
something small and shiny to bring me luck.

Back in the lines I lie and dream awhile,
take a photo from my coat, see her smile.

John Plevin

That Place

Our roof was broad
and hands of vine
heavy with dark grapes
sheltered us.

We two
I forget the exact year
or what we said
an arbour built on valley side
where time stood still.

Rustic table and benches
and across the river
forest stretched its greenness
we drank champagne in
crystal glasses clinking.

River, sun, leaves,
their shadows dancing
before us, I remember it all
do you?

Teta

February 1972

Dry-throated I awake to feel the
  brittle desert of my mind
    I fingered the (near) past all
Gritted and uncomfortable
Widespread.

Every region had its itchy coat
  butter rolled in sand
Heated and flowed to creamy abrasion.

The recent thorn has set in
  its bloodied slot.
To dwell within its swollen
    scarlet gown.

Mike Ennion

Physics

Physics! Physics! Physics!
Oh! Damn physics,
Here, there and everywhere,
There is physics and only physics.

My dad loves physics
And I hate physics,
Because it needs understanding
And which is what, I find demanding.

When I watch a match of cricket
And get foxed by their bowling tricks,
In that also, my dad says,
It is nothing but only physics.

I think I like biology
Because, there is no physics in it,
But, here too, my dad says, living bodies make up matter
And thus the part of physics.

I say chemistry consists only
Of chemical reactions,
But in that also, there are atoms
And the moment you reach atoms,
You reach in the realm of physics.

At times I wonder!
How do we walk and how do we stand?
The answer is, just because of friction and gravity,
But oh! That is also physics!

I think, the laws of mathematics
Resemble somewhat with the laws of physics
And to my dismay! Papa says,
'There is no mathematics without physics
And no physics without mathematics.'

Once, I was writing something,
Just to check my new fountain pen
And here too, because of surface tension,
There is a capillary flow, and
'That is the physics,' said Papa,
With a very wide glow.

Now I really banged my head
And said, 'Oh! Dear Physics
Please leave me alone,
With my sweet music.'
'But no! This time,' the Physics said,
'Music is sound and sound is energy,
And energy is my dearest 'Prachi';
Nothing but only physics.'

Prachi Moharir M Bajaj

Black Cloud

He will not enter the arena
Again without fear
Time has corrupted courage
Stolen strength
Foundered the fleet.

The certainty of acknowledgement
Win or lose is no more
Uncertainty floods the mind
Overreaches the head
Like an ocean wave
Indecision cripples action
Self-respect drains

No more parades
No more anthems
No more salutes

Do not hand him the short sword
Do not tape his hands
Do not tell him the bull is good
But reserve him a seat
High in the stand
Where he can watch
The Green Pyramid
Advance on the Haka.

Patrick Daly

The Missing Piece

Ten years you've sat alone
pondering memories gone by,
your missing piece has gone
parts of you have died.

The yearn for life has withered,
fragile and lonely you sit,
sunken skin and bony hands,
hair of grey; matted and limp.

Stained nails and delicate bones,
A loose wedding ring swings to and fro,
fond memories of years gone by,
thin lips smile.

Your missing piece has gone,
you pray for your maker to call,
to join your missing piece,
to once again become whole

Kathryn Houghton

Goodbye My Child

I stood in front
Of my family and friends
Hands shaking
Tears falling without end,

I couldn't understand
I couldn't even see
The words became blurred
The paper crumpled me,

I began choking
On these words
My whispered memories
Going unheard.

A tiny hand
Took my shame
My daughter's face
Shocked with pain.

'Mummy,' she said,
'Don't be sad
My brother's gone
And he's with Dad.'

A tiny tear
Fell down her cheek
She cleared her throat
And turned to speak,

'My brother Richard
Was deaf and blind
So God took him
To be kind,

My brother was sick
Since he was born
But because we remember
He'll never be gone.'

Her tiny voice
Shook with pain
I held her tight
And spoke her name.

'Hush now Lily,
No more strife
We will see them
In another life.'

I held up the candle
She blew out the flame
Goodbye my child
Until we meet again.

Kelly Millar

Just A Dream

Running through the woods unarmed
Grabbing leaves, vines and thorns unharmed
Nature's name is nature's call
The giant pit of darkness her feet swiftly fall
The eerie echo of a woman's last breath
The chilling image of her blackened death
Rising slowly
Rising full
She drifts up high, she captures you
Inside your mind she writhes and screams
Wake up you silly woman it is just a dream.

Jessica Suter

Untitled

The grass is no longer green, nor is the sky blue.
And the stars no longer light up the night.
Home is no longer a refuge and sleep is no longer escape.
Is there really anybody out there that can save us?
Because that's how it's supposed to be isn't it?
We're supposed to fall down and be picked back up.
But how is that possible in society today, when we've gangs with knives and regular crimes?
How are we supposed to say 'comfort of our own home' when to have just that you need
alarms and five locks on the front door?
It's no longer Afghanistan we are fighting, we are raging in our own war.
The colour of your skin is no longer called just 'black', 'brown' or 'white'.
The intelligence of our generation won't accept these as way of description.
But instead opt for words with harsher meaning and take pride in their conviction.
There's no longer a line to cross, the boundary's already been pushed too far.
We no longer act with feelings taken into consideration,
Destruction becoming somewhat of a fixation.
So when does it stop?
When do we wake up and realise changes have to be made?
It's already too late for total reconstruction, but all of humanity is yet to fade.

Paige Lawson

The Folly Of Youth

The folly of youth
Full of jolly times too
Nursery rhymes, puzzles and signs
Speak of the truth sublime
Searching the grapevine
Upturning every book from every spine
Sometimes inspiration is brief
Like perspiring plants that leech
And feed the earth from whence their birth
Were but part of the unbroken cycle inert
Blessed in splendour the child's mind renders
And dismembers and endeavours with caressed touch tender

The beauty of life
That emits the glowering love like a hovering dove
To rewrite the bigger picture
Their scripted depictions so vivid
Amongst them we never grow timid

Matthew Western

In Brinscall Walks

The lights lit up the Faerie Woods
The ducks were dancing on the lake
In tie and tails immaculate
While ballgowns floated on the waves
Of that sparkling inland sea,
A purple haze descended on
The slopes of Heather Lea.
As unicorns abounded,
Lightning flashed and thunder sounded
To streams of water in the woods.
While ringing through the rafters
You could hear the sound of laughter
Of the Gods.
The wizards cast their magic spells
The wind did chime the faerie bells
Their magic number ten.
All light and sounds were dazzling
Movement in the glen.
And then the darkness vanished
And the dawn did reappear.
We wish the faeries well and
A prosperous New Year.
So going by the maxim,
That if you can, you should,
You are cordially invited
To the faerie ball in Brinscall Woods.

Saxon Knight

Magic

Is there really magic
Or is it fake
The things your parents said
Whilst you were in bed, wide awake
The monsters in the closet
Spaceships in the sky
Is it your imagination?
Are you wondering why?
Is Santa Claus real?
Can he travel the world in a night?
What about the bogeyman?
Is he just to fright?
These stories we get told
Then start to believe
Like Robin Hood and the Prince of Thieves
Have you ever seen a tooth fairy?
Or Jack Frost
Is he scary?
What about the Easter bunny . . .

Please! Now don't be funny.

Joanna Chamberlain

Teenagers

Mother's potions brewing

Teenagers
Horror of horrors age
predictably unpredictable

Teenagers
Jekyll and Hydes
The incredible sulks
Sunrise's smile

Teenagers
Eating nothing then all
Munchies comforts
Fag ends shared
Enemies then friends

Teenagers
Spendthrifts misers
Never bought
Never sold
Slamming bedroom doors
Dinners cooked surprise

Teenagers
Hormones running wild
Exhaustion's duvet unsurprised
No rise and shine
For Sundays mornings chimes
Kikin bac
Saturdays nites decline

Teenagers
At sixteens and seventeens
Such fury becalmed
Friendships tested true
Laughter shining through
Parents ridiculed embarrassment
No telling off for long
Sibling staunch harassment

Teenagers . . .

John Graham

Is There No Escape From Here?

I am alone and naked. Yet how did I get here? I had gone to see a doctor.
The details are still hazy, I can't remember where.
Where are my clothes, and wallet? They have gone without a trace.
I was lying in a coffin.
The lid not yet in place,
There was some gauze
Lying on my face.
'Who would want to harm me? I am just an unemployed youth.'
'Had I had too much to drink? Or did someone inject me? I need to know the truth?
'Is this a hospital? Did they think that I was dead?' I tried to sit up, but my head
Just felt like lead.
'What if they are going to cremate me? Surely this cannot be.
I know my name, and telephone number. What is happening to me?'
They know everything about me, but why should this be so?
Am I locked inside a crematorium? I have two days to go.
Would they inform my mum and dad, and my sister Ruth?
This cannot be possible. They need to know the truth,
There were other bodies waiting to be cremated by the flame.
Someone has done this to me, but who will take the blame?
We two are victims. We went to see his show, we like you
Gave him everything that he needed to know.
We are also trapped inside these coffins. Help us to escape from this cruel fate.
If you cannot free us, we will die upon this date. Where have they taken us?
Think too of our relatives, how they will become distraught.
Once the lids are put in place, then we shall surely die.
You are the only one who can help to save us from this fate.
Try to find a telephone, to phone the police from here, before it's far too late.

James Ayrey

Treasured Memories

Where are the seasides of long ago
Ones in memory we used to know
Pleasurable trips when young
Everything there for a day in the sun
Round the fairground would take time
Seeking rides which could be good fun
Helter-skelter, The Mouse, scenic railway,
Ghost house made us shriek with fright
Now for a gentle stroll down the prom to buy
An ice cream wolf whistles following,
Footsteps not far behind
Passing street sellers on our way all saleable
Goods neatly displayed beach accessories,
Buckets, spades, fortune teller, plying her trade
Various seafoods, cockles, mussels, prawns,
Set in disposable trays.

Sticks of rock, lollipops, popcorn also
Candyfloss, that end stall sold the lot
Down below the sands looked busy a crowd
had gathered to watch Punch and Judy
Donkeys carrying rides back and forth
Waiting children crying to have a go
Sandcastles, fortresses being built kept others amused
While dads worked hard shovelling sand for their use
Far out to sea a steamship in passing was
Belching smoke from its funnels seeming
to darken the horizon
Suddenly a heavy shower started sending
Everyone running searching for shelter
Typical summer holiday weather
These treasured memories known
The beaches played upon and loved at home
Familiar sights seen no more
Never once gave thought to leave
Desert this land for distant dreams

V Thompson

Birthday Bumps

When my birthday comes each year,
My thoughts somehow do stray,
The memories that I hold so close,
Just like my fifth birthday,
I was giddy as my friends came in,
Butterflies in my belly,
However that was sorted,
By lashings of bright green jelly,
My mother made a birthday cake,
At five it seemed quite huge,
She didn't think I'd notice,
That the adults were on the booze,
Anyway, our party games,
Were absolutely fantastic,
Even when we smashed Mum's vase,
And she got quite ballistic,
I didn't see the point though,
In that nearly drowned,
'Apple bobbing' it was called,
Life jackets weren't around,
But then they pulled me too far,
And my knickers fell straight down,
'Pass the parcel' was my favourite,
Although I never won,
'Musical chairs' was more my scene,
I had a great fat bum,
I wasn't too keen on that damn game,
'Dead fishes' it was named,
The only way that you could win,
Was switching off your brain,
Then my party ended thus,
A milestone in my life,
I've had more parties after that,
But not with so much strife.

Denise A Oldale

Prelude To Infamy

The huffing and puffing ended with the arrival of rain,
Bringing tin-pot symphonies, once again,
Through the mildewed straw.
And they would walk with him and talk of their porcine fame,
Until squalls sent them trotting back to the same
Mundane labour and home-building chore.

So he went on alone and, as wise creatures do,
Found shelter in the woods, so dark and cool.
Only he was permitted to stray from the path,
For his were the roots, the boles and grass;
As were those disputed spots – the darkest marsh,
Where fallen things rot, making it difficult to pass.

At such a place he stopped to quietly admire
Her song as she skipped lithely, crossing the briar.
On her way to the cottage in the gnarly-moss wood,
Attending to the family, as he understood.
The long, sweet song pierced through the chatter
Of staccato bird noises and other such matter.

There she appeared in her little red hood
And there she stopped, and being ever so good,
Curtsied and gave compliments upon the size
Of his long sharp teeth and his doleful eyes,
Before waving, quite sweetly and rejoining the trail;
Singing where she left off and dancing away.

When the rain clouds cleared and the sun reappeared,
He strolled out to where his kind were still feared.
A boy there, he heard, had called out his name;
In warning, he screamed it, over and again.
With the sun sliding slowly down a blood-red sky,
He dropped to his fours. It was time to call by.

Simon Morgan

Encased (The Bride In The Oak Trunk)

The trunk
In the attic room
Stands in the sun;
Stroked in strands
Through dancing dust:
Waits for the child-bride
Playing hide-and-seek;
Invites her into
The secret space,
And closes her
Into silence

David Burl

A True Sense Of Escape

Mind traveller who creates life from imagination
Unlimited dream space fantasy maker
Descriptive words produce lines for expanding thoughts
Emotional trauma, epic journey, destination unknown
Feelings of love and anger unwind dramatically
Written simultaneously ending on direct poetic paths
Visibly connecting a true sense of escape.

Nigel Astell

River Rush

Seams of bright water, what shimmers beneath?
Rushes from mountain, seeps in from the heath.

A door bursts open, above a natural spring,
A call from her father, the Poseidon King.

Light twinkles its magic, she glows downstream,
Shards shine down, revealing her gleams.

She skips over, water cress and slips past a rock,
Never trips or falls, in a slippery frock.

Cool pools are still, they stare at her rush,
Her wake floods past, in a white foaming gush.

Sounds gurgle, trickle currents with force,
Can't stop her surge, no stopping her course.

She looks up to see, blue skies for her way,
In her rush, her path bursting with spray.

Sunshine's through, mosaicked speckled discs,
Sudden currents filter, the water it frisks.

Pebbles stand huddled, waiting for her flood,
Waiting for excitement, in amongst mud.

She leaps over depths, she avoids any sides,
Oh how she moves, oh how she glides.

Her curves, dome the ridge, before a waterfall,
Water is leaping, gravity enthralled.

She jumps down so quickly, he misses a trick,
This girl is so lively and ever so slick.

Her bubbles crash down, spread out in the pool,
A hot summer's day, a trout observes, in the cool.

Drinking from rain, small streams, that she passed,
Picking up speed, her power is vast.

She smiles at her nature, they need her so much,
Play within her, drink with her, but never to touch.

Onward, downwards rushing, a magnet for seas,
No pollution today no hindrance, no wheeze.

Swirly, whirly, dress glimpsed, her magical vortex,
Eyes will be fooled her illusion cortex.

Shimmer the greens, she's dressed to the nines,
Emeralds that lure, a dress so divine

Glimmering golds, long hair shines under a silver crown,
Young hair, tousled back over a meandering gown.

She runs these shadowy corridors, always in a rush,
Water irises move when her gown gently brushed.

Passing them quickly, dashing for the seas,
Her path is so familiar, under tall swaying trees.

She senses her father, is near the path open to the sea,
She'll soon be with him, dancing with glee.

He is solid like a wall, she runs to his embrace.
Now she's less restricted, a lovely open space.

He lifts her up, as she giggles her father she adores,
To sandy depths they flow away from, these rocky shores.

Meia Allegranza

Daydreaming Butterfly

Daydreaming butterfly upon a flower
You love to rest your wings of violet blue,
Today is a present, a gift to you,
You love to daydream in the bright warm sun,
You love to listen to the birds' song so sweetly sung,
You dance on air, secrets of spring you love to share,
The gentle breeze blows kisses your way,
In each bright warm sunny day,
Spring holds the key to your happiness, butterfly princess.

Joanna Maria John

Keyboard Romance

Tried computer
Online dating;
Found a suitor;
Not long waiting.

Sense of humour,
Very sporting;
Had to do more
Online courting.

Started getting
Very pally;
Heavy petting
- Virtu-ally!

Website humming;
News is spreading
Of our coming
Cyber wedding.

Clicked on 'File' as
Male and female
Wed in style as
Quick as email.

Clicked on 'Copy'
Hoping – maybe -
For a floppy
Cyber baby!

Dennis W Turner

Old Ken

He always seemed old to me did Old Ken
That's what I called him right from being little
Not to his face, but just referred, related to him, as Old Ken
It must have been thirty years or so since I had seen him
I called in to see my mum on one of my, far to infrequent visits to Leeds, from that other city
two hundred miles down the M1 that goes by the name of London
He stood at the gate of his house, near the dustbins, stood, staring into space
I thought I should go and say hello
As I got closer I slipped on the newly formed ice on the road surface
Torvill and Dean would have been proud of my ability to remain upright
thinking that he would recognise me, although I didn't know why he should, I got closer and
saw that he was wearing an old T-shirt with trousers of the same vintage.
Clothes tattered by time to match his face
The years had not been kind to him
He was crying, not crying, he was sobbing
Feeling inadequate I turned and gingerly walked back across to my mum's house
I told her what I had just experienced and, in a moment of lucidity and without a trace of
sorrow in her voice she said, 'His wife died a couple of days ago, he's been like that a lot.'
I said to her, 'You should have told me.'
She retorted sharply, 'I thought everyone around here knew.'
It didn't seem right to remind her where I lived and maybe I shouldn't remind her.

Ray Tough

Hope

When you are so tired and lonely too
And you are not too sure of what to do
Think, you are loved for being you.
When you smile you change the world
It's a far better place
For when you smile and give out love
No one can take your place.

Love is trust
down the years
Hope, trust, despite the tears
Joy is friendship, strong and true
Peace is when they meet in you
Kindness we need when things go wrong
A song in our heart to keep us strong
So my child I give to you
Love, joy. And peace and wisdom too.

Trevor A Mercer

Richard

an abandoned park
such as parks
are left to decay
young trees take over
the paths the lawns

the toad becomes a monster
fowl are fishers
of an abandoned lake
the eye of the magpie
bass big as a dish

Richard is a boy
with an iron heart
he makes his followers
crawl in the grass
at his bidding

Richard leads the boys
on hands and knees
through a tunnel
formed of dead grass
Richard's escape route

the tunnel winds about the park
it has many branches
Richard is fearless
as a boy of ten
with power over others

a blood red sun
dips as Richard enters his tunnel
Richard's followers
are reluctant to succeed him
Richard plunges through the tunnel

Richard exults in leadership
is strong where others are weak
the boys have stayed
they do not know
what goes on in the park

the great eye of the magpie
is consuming Richard's efforts
working the other boys
to a pitch of self-delusion

of gang membership

the park bull
has escaped its tether
raises Richard on its horns
the ten year old's body
describes a fine arc

thud Richard hits the ground
gashed eyes wide open
Richard's followers smile
they know Richard
was too fine to live

Simon Warren

A Rock Named Colour

Born from stone,
Roll tumbling cliffs,
Carved by aerial artists.
And from the rough
Fell a single rock,
Encrusted with jewels and diamonds.
The rock was named 'Colour'
And sparkled with splendour,
Blinding people with wonder.

And in bloody fog,
Greed and envy,
The rock itself was stolen.
Removed from its sacred place
By bands of men who
Killed to carry its beauty.

But fight not for Colour -
As it is Heaven's pleasure,
And Earth's sacrificial gem-child.
A gift bestowed for the worthy
To view
With a collective conscience.
No one man's to have -
And no one man's to hold,
Colour is there forever.

Stuart Russell B.E.M

Physical Jerk

Paddling down that river in a canoe
Builds up those biceps
Running twenty-six miles in a marathon
You're working on those thighs

You've got to swim that channel
To make all your muscles
Supple, shiny and bulging
Till they burst

You get on that exercise bike
And go that extra mile
So you're ready for the Tour de France

You're a physical jerk
An exercise berk
You've gotta keep in shape
Even if it kills you

Lift those weights
Banish all those calories
Steroid hell

Keep fit in the gym
Dance till you drop
To the music that will drive you mad

Karate king
Aggressive sport of hate
But the bigger they are
The harder they fall

You're a physical jerk
An exercise berk
You've gotta keep in shape
Even if it kills you

Mutley

Assassin

He was like any person
you might meet in the street.
Not too inconspicuous,
not too neat.
He couldn't stand out,
be noticed in a crowd.
He had to blend in;
he couldn't be too loud.
His intention was obscurity;
not wanting to be seen.
He couldn't be remembered
in the place where he had been.
He had but one intention,
one purpose on his mind;
to kill his chosen victim
and leave no trace of him to find.
To disappear into the night
and never again be seen.
This was his profession,
a specialist killing machine.
He could be your neighbour,
a friend you met in the park.
Take care how you treat people.
You might be his next mark.

Tom Maxwell

The Changing Times Of Nature

The times are changing daily no doubt so slowly and surely
We must search for the meaning and purpose of our lives
As we have no time to stand and stare at past times
We live in the present and we tend to moan betimes
There are times we forget and easily forego the past
Nearer comes the time we long for and we gloat aghast
When where we are now is just a taste of future fantasy

The time we were born is past in time and now points to death
Which may come prematurely or late at our Maker's will
Imagine the life span of trees, the fishes – they also live and die
The camels and kangaroos, king lion, the snakes and the fly
Nature is hard at work for all of our existence and extinction
We must not reflect on past times without acknowledging our actions
For the future days are carefully numbered with each fleeting breath

'The world is a stage' what a true adage now and forever
We are merely playing our part in time past and future
Let us stop and think that lights out point to a change of scene
So do what you can to move with the times and stay absolutely clean
For the times are fast changing in this precious and fleeting world
Today you are here – high or low, rich or poor the truth is unfurled
Tomorrow you are gone – time is up – for in dust your body lies ever

Goodbye means the future is here present and time has far gone
The music has ended and so must the dance stop in present time
As the day began with the rising sun, night appears with the bright moon
Darkness appears changing the scene from light to dark – oh how soon!
Our lights are distinguished when we least expect in present time
The end of time is here and now like the beginning we hope it's fine
Life ebbs away so soon as it began when as babe we were born

Rebecca Ada Williams

The Modern Writer(s)

So I stare onwards and at nothing,
and still I wait.
For an idea worth questioning myself over.
Something that feels like
my work
can do it justice.

And if it's this hard
really
I should give it up.
There's no dialogue in the thoughts,
and it'll end up rough and with no flow.
Yes,
just like that.
Flow doesn't happen here.

There are no flourishes of a quill
or beads of ink settling
sinking deeper into the pores of a page.
Scrawled permanence.
True literature.
Just a screen-blank void
where things clunk into place
and flit out again.

Some odd part of me needs it though.
When I think of how many
others must be doing the same
it feels unreal. I don't want them to struggle
harder than me.
I want to be the one who channelled the bad ideas
in the best way.

So I stare onwards, with purpose, with need.
I won't be the one who settles.
And though there are so many others
who do the same and who I do not know,
they go on, with their doubts too, I suppose.

Josh Moorby

Creative Thoughts

I remember it was a lasting moment.
Memorable it remained.
It was a time of innocence.
Everything was new and fresh.
I craved for knowledge.
I longed to explore the unknown.
My thirst for knowledge enabled me to grow.
It was a time when I was young and innocent.
I was a child.

I packed my suitcase with an air of foreboding, because life can be overwhelming.
And I often get flustered
But I take a step back
To regain my focus
Then everything seems
Clear once again
I remember I was broken into pieces
Imperfect was my reflection
But I was able to admit it
And willing to discover
What life has to offer?
I packed my suitcase with nostalgia and I remember that this was my last time in my old house.
My father built it for me and my brothers from brick by brick and layer by layer.
This I know it will always be home.
My dad liked dogs and my mom preferred cats
So we had loads of pets around the house.
These are a few of the things I remember.

Ise Obomhense

Alive – An Empty Plate

Barefooted
starving eyes
unable to deal successfully with the situation
a lost soul . . .
unable to understand because it was too complicated

lost in thought . . .
an innocent young girl
she couldn't leave herself to starve to death
I wished, I owed her an apology for what she was feeling
I wished . . .
I owed everything to her
she wore shabby clothes and her feet were bare
It seemed, she like to walk around in bare feet
empty mind
the eyes were completely bare
she was short of even the bare necessities of life
a girl with empty hands
an empty plate
she stood staring emptily into space
she emptied her mind of all thoughts of home and food?
She looked sad and tired
I felt terribly sad about it
she sat for hours just gazing into space
staring into space silently
food
lots of food
she looked at them with dark staring eyes
so many questions on my mind
and the answer was staring her in the face
she dropped her gaze
it seems she had her own secluded garden
to lead a secluded life
she lived almost entirely secluded from the public gaze
a broken window of her soul
a broken plate
with broken hope
she was seeing full of living things
all moving things
with her tired mind
she had to steal food just to stay alive
It was a perfectly innocent drama

a hunger . . .
ah, an event caused by natural forces
beyond human control
an act that
aware of reality
knowing the exists and is importance of things
to be alive to the dangers
facts
possibilities
responsibilities
WFP (World Food Programme)
WFC (World Food Council)
UNICEF (United Nations Children's Fund)
And she looked at them with dark staring eyes!

(There's still some hope of making a bad situation better
all isn't lost!)

Ushna Sardar

A Feast For The Oblivious

Dirty savage, a cannibal
eating away at sweet flesh.
Flesh.
The flesh of the shattering shells,
the small spreads, the bodies.
Inside, slurps of the blood, the blood,
the guts and the blood.
Turning pink to blue. White.
He grows growling and petrifies.
I am stone.
Stone cold of little hope, what with fate.
Ugly fate.
The shock. The terror as I watch.
Look how it smiles and expands,
its greatness looks down with triangular canines.
Her blood is tainted,
her face weak,
her body weak.
Weak with fate and the happenings of the uncontrollable.
Something I call fate. The brute!
The trickles of her life dripping into his salivating mouth, like when water cleans blood.
But here, blood dirties water.
It wipes away her smile, her life, her smiling smile, full of life with her smile.
A cannibal.
Eating her alive, inside to out.
Nearing the flesh and the skin, her internals far gone.
I'm on my knees now, hands pressed like a mass grave.
I pray now.
Then something greater.
Something I call God.
Salvation.

Carys Tellyn

Lust

Like April's soft sun
Upon my skin. Close my eyes
Your kisses are indulgent
Travelling inwards, upwards
Lost in pleasure's maze

Touch me. Without contact
My mind became less
My words lacked life.
Nothing to liken my similes

Daniels. Told me your
First name was Jack
Like the thief in the night
You stole my innocence
But I was arrested

For aiding and abetting
So drunk on your love.
I couldn't make out the
Difference between
Jay and Bee -

Beyond your touch I was
Lost. Drowning in lust
Tripped and fell in
Love with your touch
High on your scent

The curve of your smile left me
Drowsy while elated
And excited. Like ecstasy
Illegal and deadly
You are forbidden fruit

For when I eat you I
Die. A thousand deaths.
Grunts of exhaustion
Daydreams of you thrusting
In and out of my mind. I
Need a drink. Thoughts of you
Leave me thirsty.

Tumi Mary Taiwo

Why?

Questions became interrogations
Everything sensationalised
A step became a trek
Flecks and specks became pools of blood.
Each from a hidden source, a locked box where the only key was PE sessions where the
teach would ask
What's that on your wrist?
Sweatbands, wristbands, hairbands, watches might cover the splotches on your skin
but not the tears in your life

We didn't cry but screamed
Except it seemed that all was fine
Like sadness is something you can get a cream for
Or sow the seams of the skin back together
Just take it on the chin and
Get over it

Carefully plaster the scars after and pretend it's a love bite
Tell them that you fell in a rosebush
Say
I wonder where that's from
Until they leave
Until they go away and stop asking you why
Because you can't reply but they can't stand by and watch this happen.
So you lie

You're scared of how they will react when you tell them
The reason you attacked yourself was
Not because you were an ugly duckling or because no one would f**k you
Not because you're stressed, or depressed or distressed or because your favourite teacher
tried to undress you or because you're possessed by the Devil or not blessed by God or
because you're messed up with depression or you feel pressurised by everything so much
so that you feel like you are being compressed into a hole.

So, why?

Rosie Richards

Goodbye Mrs Jamison

I arrived on the platform with the other evacuees
With a bag in my hand and two unwashed knees
I held my young sister's hand as we came as a pair
Not wanting to let go to show that I care

People arrived taking other children without a fuss
We stood there alone, scared, just the two of us
A lady came up to say all the places were taken
The emotions inside were finally awaken

A single tear slowly slaloming from my watery eye
My sister turned, 'Brother, please don't cry'
The lady hugged me and said, 'We'll sort something out'
We turned suddenly as we heard an almighty shout

Mrs Jamison quickly came over and apologised for being late
She was short with dark hair and didn't carry much weight
We signed the forms and she took us both by the hand
We were excited to be travelling across new untouched land

We stopped at a house with a garden in the front and back
And greeted by an older boy who Mrs Jamison called Jack
It was her youngest son, who worked tirelessly on the farm
He asked us excitedly if we would like to play in the barn

Mrs Jamison undoubtedly became our forever Welsh mother
And her son, Jack, like a new older brother
News from back home would arrive once a week
Bombing raids and blackouts made it sound rather bleak

Then one day we were told the war was finally over
No more German planes would fly over the White Cliffs of Dover
Peace at last and we could go back home to the city
Our goodbye to Jack and Mrs Jamison seemed so very bitty

We kept in touch by letter throughout the many years
Until one day a letter would bring on the heartbreaking tears
Mrs Jamison, God bless her, had sadly passed silently away
I will always be thankful she came on that evacuation day

And now I'm eighty-five I can still remember her name
She never wanted thanks or even craved fame
When my mother passed away she was the first to be in touch
Even now I want to tell her that I loved her so much

Darren Partington

A Place To Be?

I close my eyes and drift into a dream
Of places, where I would like to be.
Somewhere, where I can see the sea,
Where there is a bustling bay,
And I can see the boats as they go on their way.
Or, down where the trade winds play with
The palm trees, make them sway -
Or I'm on a gondola in Venice, no less!
Or France, to sit on a beach in Nice, that's nice!
Maybe, I'm at a fiesta, that's a delight and
The dancing to music, a gay sight and then
I awake, I open my eyes, I know of a place!
That is right – a seat by the fireplace, a
Book on my knees, and you my love
Bringing in cups of tea.
So never again, in a dream, will I roam
'Cause, the best place for me, is here, in our home.

Jo Mackenzie

Ragnar's Tooth

So the ancient ones say, night may soon conquer day, though our Mighty Protector still stands.

But as time passes by, he might wither and die, and the darkness will cover our land.

Then a hero must rise, blazing truth fills his eyes, with pure goodness and strength in his heart.

With a quest he must make, there's a journey to take, so Sleepy Dog Land will not fall apart.

To Ragnar's Tooth he must go, a fabled land deep below, where the black river flows to the sea.

Sacrifice must be made, for the treasure he'll trade, granting life to the Happiness Tree.

If the tree once more stands, dark must flee from our land, as the roots of protection re-form.

Once the magic's bestowed, to satisfy ancient codes, only then Sleepy Dog Land's reborn.

Hilton Eros Eros James

My Footsteps

Lord let me follow in your footsteps let me be as one with you,
Lead me out of the darkness show me the light from you,
Take away my doubt show me the road I must take,
To your heavenly kingdom that after this life I must take,
Let me spread the gospel of your Holy name as I kneel and pray to you and spread your
Holy fame.

Lord show me the way to righteousness,
Forgive all my earthly sin as I take the path with you please cleanse my soul within,
As I take your pathway you will be my guide for I know you walk with me as you are always
by my side,
Bring me out of darkness show me your guiding light so that I may be as one with you and
only do what's right.

Lord give me strength of purpose to carry out your task
Help me on this long road is to you all I ask,
Show me the road to freedom as I spread your Holy name,
Grant us peace on Earth away from war and shame.

Lord let me follow in your footsteps let me be as one with you,
Lead me out of the darkness show me the light from you.

Roy Muir

Pere

And was life's tree of knowledge harvest sued,
Which bowed to robe in fruit at Pere's unfold,
That came like gold by reap to Eden's brood,
To woman's man by pair's pluck would hand hold.
So good and evil on a branch was grasp,
Where then two hands did clasp a fruit in sight,
Which held a sinless right in Serpent's rasp?
Though this bold pair were Pere's own likeness quite.
Yet 'fore a fig des-pair bore bitter grieves,
Eve did a rape in pare bare from this tree,
That made a pair in suit to prepare leaves,
Which did a pair in wore now Ficus be.
For never was a pear in reap's behold,
More than the pair in sound but not its mould!

Barry Bradshaigh

More Crumbs!

(Based On Matthew 15: 7-29 And Mark 7: 16-31 KJV)

As to rituals of hygiene
Separating Gentiles and Jews
Jesus knew at the Sidon scene
Of cross-cultural worship views
How dirty hands easily clean
While hypocrites' hearts stay obscene.

When a Greek pled at Christ's eardrums
That her girl be not possessed,
Although then somewhat distressed
By His test of birth-rights to Grace,
She claimed that curs could have crumbs
And that disclosure won her case.

Outside Jewish jurisdiction
Christ was taught, then told His band
Tradition made their kind blind
And His death by crucifixion
Would fulfil what God planned;
One saving faith for humankind.

Ronald Rodger Rodger Caseby

Help Me To Start Again

In a pool of pain and bitterness,
Comforted by contrition and unexplainable love,
I looked into the skies with my hands high . . .
I closed my naked eyes and asked why.

I have been here before . . . I'm here again,
Same gathering in the same demented atmosphere,
A kind-hearted dove that mingles with the cassowaries . . .
A familiar start with a predicted end.

Why did I flee from You O Lord!
Why is this path so cold O Lord!
My father prayed . . . my mother wept!
Help me O Lord to start again!

Now I claim that pain is hope
As sunrise is far and its light so faint.
Once played a saint but now a villain
As the story is told again and again.

As his wrinkle strengthens and brags,
As her fine black hair turns to grey,
The flesh still in the gathering and did not understand . . .
The spirit looks down and shakes his head.

Ndidi Ubogu

Across Normandy's Sands

Forward to guns through fire and pain,
With thunder in their souls and a passion that won't wane,
In the hundreds they fell to breathe no more,
Their first and last tastes of the horrors of war,
Young boys and men together they stand,
Pushing forward for freedom across Normandy's sands,
The echoes of cannons and their fallen brethren's last gasps,
These images are not the ones that should last,
Our future our life our every existence,
We owe everything to those who lost it all in an instance,
With daughters and wives and mothers left at home,
Many thousands of men bravely stood and died alone,
The land that we stand on, the flag covered in blood,
Of those who won't hear their grandchildren cry as they should,
Millions of bodies lie lifeless and still,
Yet the horrors of war, unending, haunt us still,
Let the fire of war spark into us new thought,
Of those who sacrificed everything, those whom have fought,
Let them not fade into meaningless extinction,
Deliver their message, their defining distinction,
One of courage and bravery that will stand the test of time,
Giving us freedom for everything, for your life and mine.

Antony Aiken

Ridiculous

Have you ever quarrelled with a building?
Or mourned with a tree?
Neither have I,
Because that's stupid.

But what if they could talk and walk?
Dance and sing and all sorts?
If a table could fight
Or a flower could cry
Maybe things would improve.
Think about it -
A garage sighing
A lamp post lying
A machine gun laughing
A bicycle clapping
How much brighter does the world seem?

Ridiculous.

Charlie Christodoulou

Battle Scars

These scars so dear to me
no judgement befallet thee.
No secret no shame I am free
laid bare for all to see,
worn with happiness and glee.

Badge of honour worn with valour,
wars that are won, those undone, some to come.
As warnings they stare at you, a judgement for ones they slew.
They pierced one's skin bled within
hidden far from one's own kin.
They bear one's joy, one's faith and hope
A dwindling soul has helped them cope.

Armour of love from below and above
to walk in pride and never ever hide,
shame and disgraced they have erased
no secret to share, someone cared.
Battle scar, a strength in war.

Earthchild

Little Me

Do you see what what's hidden beneath me
No as your soul is caged and not free
Do you even know how to be honest and true
No you don't see what your lies do
Do you know how pure this heart is and you will never compare
No because your jealousy doesn't allow you to share
Do you know I'm so unique but you think of me as dust
No because you see my worth no more than your car's rust
Do you know I'm clear as the air and water
No because you see me as nothing not even your daughter
Do you accept that one day I'll succeed
No because you refuse to plead
You can't see through your own hatred and disgust
Lost in your own life not love nor lust
Your bitterness has evaded the heart you once had
But I refuse any longer to feel sad
I just want to write and keep going strong
As this road I'm travelling is so very long
It's going to lead me to the place I need to go
So right now I'm taking it nice and slow
Do you know I'm not fragile or weak
No because that's what you choose to seek
Do you know I'm worth more than the stars in the sky
No because your eyes can't see that high
What I do know is that you can boast about your wealth
But I value something deeper that's greater, it's my health
You can be the one to stand in the crowd
I'd rather stand back but still stand proud
I just want to live and be happy and free
Just to live a life and just be me

Sharena Satti

A Place To Go

Familiar, yet oddly strange,
this is a place you may freely range.

Wear those rose-tinted spectacles
to see what you can see,
to help you sidestep obstacles
wherever you may be.

Your head held high in cloud, look out
for castles in the air.
Cuckoos will find them, no doubt,
that has bedrooms to spare.

Settle there for pie in the sky
and enjoy that cloudscape.
After watching many pigs fly,
back down to Earth, escape.

To play about with platitudes
a positive pleasure.
Somehow, they reveal attitudes
that enlighten leisure . . .

Familiar, yet oddly strange,
this is a place you may freely range.

Chris Creedon

If Eyes

If eyes were stars,
a soul to ponder within,
to look through almighty scars,
of every deed and every sin.

If eyes were tears,
a hose to dwell the rights,
and mark all craving fears,
for peace to end all fights.

If eyes were scales,
to balance the bolts of life,
encounter every human race,
what law of guns and knives?

If eyes were flames,
first to burn all equality,
and live the chance of desired aims,
for the world to seek all hidden humanity.

If eyes were diverse shades,
from tinted tones and all,
the colours off emerald-jade,
or specks of a brown dust wall.

If eyes once lay,
within tiresome lines of hope,
and a promise will forever stay,
amid the jagged rope.

Amina Abuzaid

Scorned

I am the goddess, I am the fire
I am the one whom your men desire
I carry wisdom, I digest truth
It's an eye for an eye, a tooth for a tooth
I am the listener, I am the light
I am the one you will miss at night
I am strength, I am alive
I am the one that washes clean with the tide
I am the winds, I am the moon
Who casts magic on darkness yet is gone all too soon
You let me go, you cut the ties
You fed me nothing but poison and lies
But I rise like a phoenix, out of the ashes I fly
Growing stronger and better with less reason to cry

Dawn Jones

Warning Signs

We have so many warning signs
No politician will heed
Political incompetence moving at speed,
Most not succeed,
World population need some creed,
Depravation and poverty a growing breed,

Sadly, life is moving in the wrong direction
If luck's on your side you have protection,
On the wrong side and lose direction.

We've lived with fraud and corruption
And offshore banking to hide
No justice system to cover our pride,
Freedom of speech a lost cause
Freedom of information, their gain not ours,

Warning signs costing us the Earth
Casting problems on young from birth,
They must wake up to political temerity
To combine their worth for prosperity.

Barbara R R Lockwood

Metaphysical Sour Grapes

Samuel Johnson knew his stuff, no doubt about it
The dictionary was special and lifted the nation
So at what I say now please don't throw a fit
His sharp observation and venerable station
Gave him no right to slander the poet John Donne
If wooing young ladies required some bloody flea
And got them into bed I'd say job was well done
Sounds like our 'Tetty' hadn't answered Sam's plea
Sour grapes back then were the name of the game
Not getting enough and someone's frustrated
Let's take it out on John! He'd far too much fame
His pious reflection well that's also overrated
Common sense I applied if and when I go wooing
Mature ones are best, they know what they're doing

Charles Keeble

Give

In this world of loving and living
There's not much time
For giving
Giving your time to others
Why care?
Giving your money
Why share?
Giving your heart to comforting,
Those in pain, and grief,
To give instead of take
Is something to believe in,
Believe in this world
That was made by Man,
Believe in those people
You cannot understand
Because you don't know them,
Doesn't mean you should not care,
Can't you spare a few moments
Of your time to share,
Share someone's troubles,
Give them some help, some hope.
Don't just give up and give in,
Try to help the world,
The world we all live in.

Trudie Sullivan

Robert Naylor

Robert Naylor was a fine singer,
And, in my mind memories do linger,
A fine tenor voice had he,
I was an amateur singer you see,
He put me through it and it had to be,
The finest tenor Robert was he,
Still forgotten after over forty years,
Yet he was world famous I hear,
He was England's highest-paid tenor of all time,
Earning £500-£1,000 which wasn't a crime,
A lot of money in the days of yore,
And, deserved earnt when people didn't want more,
Today I'm sad to mention, when he passed away,
He had no media attention.

Pauline Wood

Life On The Street

Out there a child cries with hunger
Out there a baby's left abandoned
Out there a girl searches for her family
Out there an old man weeps
Out there a frail woman seeks friendship.

That's a picture of life on the street in many great cities.
Unforeseen, despair lingers
Search for food and shelters all that matters.
Faded rainbow predicts a bleak tomorrow
Crushing someone further into the gutter
Academic and scientific knowledge,
Mingled with material want
Deprives the mind of the exploration of knowledge
Silently stealing dignity.
Exit obscured
Only God's mercy can point the way to a new beginning
A brighter future
Away from the degrading life
Life on the street.

Frances Gibson

The Bungalow

It is a little place, situated
In an old people's complex
Called Saltisford Gardens.
It is home to me now,
Ever since I relapsed at my house
In the village of Whitnash
And was admitted to St Michael's Psychiatric Hospital.

A year I languished, in the wards,
I went through a violent phase,
But was looked after by a beautiful
Asian woman, a consultant psychiatrist.
She was slim and tall with dark
Olive skin and long back hair.
'I can't stand it Doc!' I shouted
At one consultation.
However, not once did I even think
Of running off. They used to let me out
On a Sunday, to go to church on my own.
The big historic church of St Mary Collegiate,
In Warwick. I would look at the tomb
Of Thomas Beauchamp, in full armour,
With his wife, Catherine Mortimer.
He was commander at the Battle of Crecy,
Then in the Beauchamp chapel,
Beside the tomb of Richard Beauchamp,
I would offer up prayers for the patients.
He was custodian of Rouen Castle,
During the imprisonment of Joan of Arc.
Then I would walk the four miles
Back to the hospital – the nurses saved me dinner!
The consultant found the right drugs
To put me on, and I hope against hope
Came the day of my discharge . . .
She found me a bungalow from the council,
Where I can live and be free. I just have

To go to hospital once daily,
To collect my drugs – just half a mile away.

I have lived in the bungalow
Several years now, I give thanks
To God for my new home.

R O'Shaughnessy

December Sky

Chill winds cut like a knife edge
shimmering frost made leaf patterns on the bonnet
of grey-green Rover: ice stung the air like a demented wintry bee
till fingers froze in sympathy
bitter winds bite, no respite
to bear a searing pain of loneliness
isolation, ice-kissed windowpanes, pavements, streets,
easterly wild winds soughed, growing
like a roaring lion
winter's arrival
freezing frost-numbed senses
echoing each lost, lonely heart . . .
ephemeral grey days, bright lights behind drawn curtains
dull nights drinking mulled wine
dulling sense and reason
dusk brooded then night like a vulture swoops
claiming its own, every bird flown to its nest
I draw the curtains, certain it will drop to minus zero

September, I remembered was bittersweet
11th the darkest day, the blackest night
in memory's mists of time
now icy icons mirror coldness reflected
in frozen faces without hope
I wished for spring; when will we breathe,
hear singing of the birds?
Skeletal trees stand stark in lacy patterns
of a bleak December day
as Christmas crashes with an anticlimax.

Judy Studd

The Clearness

Standing in amongst the still clear water
Darting fish weave in awe, around, glowing white flesh beneath a fierce sun.
Caressing skin like lovers,
Freed silky mossy green algae floats like ghosts, slides off my legs and back on again, teasing, provoking.
There is no sound of waves or birds.
(This must be what Heaven feels like).
The stillness, the silence
and the solitude. Shush, shush, shush.
(I can hear my breathing).
The hot sun does not waiver, beats down on stung shoulders, hits the unmoving body of,
Deep turquoise aquamarine blue topaz water, and bounces back again, in a shock of brightness that can hurt, so,
(I close my eyes).
I feel cocooned, enveloped in smooth coolness, and, I go further in.
It is home and I go slow.
I go further in and sink, below, another world.
I open my eyes and shut things out, the quietness of it surrounds my bare skin, there is nothing else.
Merged union sea and me, never sure of a start or a finish. I am hypnotised by his touch.
I go further in.

Caro Bushnell

Bogeyman

Oh the bogeyman that we all fear,
But do we know him at all?
For we do everything to avoid him
But don't say, scared of being the fool!

Is he the being who hides in the shadows,
Or the person who talks behind one's back?
Then there's those who stare and disappear,
As don't ask, how are we meant to know, facts!

What about those shadows we can't explain,
Or you've lost something, was it taken by Him?
Something falls unexpectedly with a horrific bang,
Now *paranoid* why is the unexplained so grim?

A flash of light or a noise that makes you jump,
Or he's in the reflection that gives you a fright?
Hiding in darkness that gives an unnerving effect,
Scream, 'Bogeyman's found me,' when woken suddenly at night!

Do you think the Bogeyman was our own invention,
Just to hide our embarrassment of our inner fears?
Who would we blame, it's easier when it's someone else,
But life is more fun when there's bogeyman tears!

Ann Beard

A Bouquet To Flanders

Solemnly by a surging river she waits in solitude,
Her pale face kissed by moonlight,
Shimmering silver wavelets dance
And sparkle in lunar radiance,
Racing impatiently towards the sea.

Alone where once a soldier stood,
A bouquet of meadow flowers in hand,
Moist eyes glistening in moonlight,
She casts her gift upon the river,
Swiftly lost to sight
In the dark orifice of the night.

A gentle wind wafts melancholic
Sounds across the sea,
The guns of battle,
Tidings of death and putrescent,
Faceless warriors, faithful souls,
Across the Fields of Flanders.

A solitary bouquet bobbed upon the sea,
Swept away by the running tide,
A messenger of love to a soldier,
Standing proud in freedom's fight,
Or lying still draped in Death's cloak
Hidden beneath the dark shadows
Of the night.

Richard Kinsella

My Fair Isle

England, oh England! My fair isle.
I like your flair, I like your style.
From your castle tall to your cottage small,
I love and appreciate one and all.
Each season boasts your flora green,
From your city verges to your village green.
How I love to spend a day,
Amongst the bluebells in the month of May.
And watch the farmers at harvest time,
Bringing in the hay.
The scent of Christmas is in the air,
Chestnuts roasting in Leicester Square.
One day I'll rest beneath your soil,
But I hope it's not for quite a while.

Maria Currey

Sunday Roast

I'm a hot potato,
And this is my jacket.
All crispy and yellow,
Bake me in a croquette.

When making Sunday Roast,
You do me golden brown.
I will raise you a toast
And you can chomp me down.

Kavita Kulkarni Frary

Herald The Day

Herald the day when we are all free
From racism, sexism and all conformity
When we finally learn to be ourselves
Without trying to fit in with the world

When families are no longer hungry
And we are all free from mental slavery
It's hard to turn on the news and see
There are people out there worse off than me

When we can finally put war to an end
When we can all learn to be friends
When good conquers over all evil ways
When we can all see better days

Mankind is his own worst enemy
His disregard for Mother Nature is a travesty
We're destroying our planet every day
So much of it is thrown to waste

We must teach our children that violence is wrong
That there are better ways to get along
We must be an example that they can follow
For they need to know the way to go

Our parents give us the skills in life
That we need in order to survive
They show us the difference between right and wrong
In order for us to carry on

When a starving child is no longer in sight
I know we are doing something right
We can make this world a better place
By not judging some by their race

If we could just free our shallow minds
It wouldn't take us long to realise
That there's room in this world for everybody
So let us come together in unity

Franklin Brady

Life's Greatest Honour

What is the most precious thing the world can bestow?
It's the love of our friends, the respect of our foe,
And if these are the things for which you have yearned,
Just remember, that these are things which have to be earned.

For nothing is worth having, if it's easy to achieve,
That's something that many folk find hard to believe,
Somehow they think that there is no need to strive,
And everything will come to them, if they just stay alive.

But in all honesty we know that this cannot be true,
Even though it may happen to just a few,
Some may be born with a silver spoon in their mouth,
But most have to struggle, of that there is no doubt.

Some may be lucky in their lives, that is true,
Having the good fortune that comes to just a few,
But the only fortune many of us ever receive,
Is the reward for the things we are able to achieve.

If we think that wealth is the only fortune, then we shall err,
There are other things more precious that we should prefer,
To be known as honest, friendly, sincere and true,
Is the greatest honour that life can bestow upon you.

Ronald Martin

Heartbeat

When hurt is deep inside
The pain burns just like a candle's flame
My heart tortures itself
I wear my heart so you can see
You left me, you didn't look back
The curtains let in the sunlight
And look around
In another new day's air
The bed is empty
Where you used to be
The days are fast behind me
Your love went cold
I had to let go of something
I couldn't hold
Memories only hurt
Pictures of you cut deep
Images come and go while I sleep
It used to make me weep
I thought some day I would belong
How could I be wrong?
I feel I can start to be strong
I feel myself standing at the window
I remember the goodbye
It made me cry
Every day a broken heart
Starts to heal
Every year I have to make do
Without you
Maybe some time
You will walk back into my life
Because goodbye cuts like a knife
Maybe we will meet again
They say blood is thicker than water
Love is fleeting
My heart has stopped beating
By the time you look for us
We will no longer exist
I will still form the morning mist
Feelings will turn to cold hard pain
It hurts to think
That right deep down you don't care
You don't question your feelings

I will never give up the fight
I will see you again
We thought we could go on no more
The battle may be lost
But not the war
When a promise is made it is kept
While a person lay dying
She must have wept
Someday the ghost of the past
Will fill you with regret
You will stand at a grave of people
You once knew
The dead will never forget
You will feel the pains of regret
My mother died not knowing
What held her hand
She longed for you to be there
She died not knowing
If you really care
We loved her
With her she took her pride
She died because
For you she could not wait
For regrets it's too late
I look at the pictures
It's a story that will not end
It's the future for us
That is at an end.

Sam Lou Grolel

To love you forever
Is my peace of mind
And I know that
You love me
For you're one of a kind

When we are together
It's oh, oh so grand
Your touch
Is like magic
When you
Hold my hand

And when we kiss
It's heavenly
For I know
Your love is true
And only you
Know the reason
There will
Never be
Another you.

Edna Holcombe

Dance In The Sun

Dance in the sun little lady
Running with the waves.
Let the Earth feel the warmth of your tiny toes.
Catch the breeze as it sings off the sea
Listen to the story in the air.

Dance in the sun little lady
Running with the waves.
The Earth feels the beat of your tiny heart.
Spinning in a dance that sets you free
In this moment without any care.

Dance in the sun little lady
Running with the waves.
This day is the longest shining just for you.
Remember the dance and let yourself be
Remember the sun on your golden hair.

Maria Potter

Emergence

The glaring, unforgiving, broken sun beats hard on the chocolate ash,
Rays bashing the black melting tarmac, smells of confusion and cut grass.
It's summertime, a reprieve so close its sweet taste dances on my seeking tongue,
Three months of promise stretch before me,
Like the toddler's balloon,
its tangibility evades my grasp.
Flying high through the clouds,
Birds soar and curve through fields of hope;
I must be my own navigator,
working through the turns of time's tiny hands.
The doors are flung open,
its hinges creak relief, salvation, joy
yet the sweeping wind's fluidity does not quite meet
with my tentative steps into the backless abyss.
Is the binding pose,
the tense limitation,
segregation from society's sauna really all so bad?
Is there really any difference, freedom can make one equally sad?
No conformism, unable to follow the ducks in what we thought was an eternal row,
Suppression gives direction,
We're no longer 'in the know'.

Sarah-Jane Coyle

Remember For Me

I look in the window
To see what I can buy
There's an old fellow
Staring back at me

I wander along the street
Don't know why I'm there
I begin to remember
1943

Beside me walks a lady
She remembers me
A smile that's kind and friendly
Full of sympathy

I'm at home now
Wherever this may be
Looking out of the window
What has happened to me?

I'm scared and alone

Kevin Jackson

Escape To Another Realm

I thought of myself as a shadow dancing to a candle's flame
Unseen in night's dark embrace
. . . Listening, watching, waiting,
Lost in the noise of life's turbulent bubbling volcano.

Moonlight created shadows of black-cloaked ghosts
That moved and existed in another world
. . . Full of stardust.
Flames on my fire rose and fell

. . . Danced with the wind,
Fireflies, splintered embers raced to the stars,
Grey smouldering ash lay on the ground
. . . Claimed by the wind.

In my solitude
I plunged into crystal-clear cold waters,
Gasped for breath,
Rose alive vibrant a three-dimensional miracle,

But I listened to the siren's song
As they moved like an ethereal mist through my mind,
Once again I became a shadow dancing to a candle's flame.
I remembered the city

With rain-soaked ebony mirrored roads,
Reflecting a kaleidoscope of multicoloured lights
Where chimneys aligned in regimented rows stood aloft,
Redundant silhouettes of a time gone by,

. . . Unmarked soot-lined gravestones.
I lay quietly in the silence listening, watching, waiting,
Stars faded as the night slowly slipped away.
The whisper of a gentle breeze played amongst unseen leaves,

Morning rose like the sound of hobnail boots
Walking through a cobblestoned courtyard,
A breeze ruffled tranquil waters
Where clouds drifted in another realm and

Chainmailed phantoms glided into a black underworld
Leaving lilies to float free from the mermaid's hair.

Frost on my breath an exorcised ghost.

David M Walford

Inspiration

On a hot summer's day with my easel in front of me,
everywhere I look there's a kaleidoscope of colour,
to inspire any landscape painter.
Suddenly streams of light filter down through the trees,
encapsulating the different
shades of green. Beside me are blue cornflowers, reminding me
of a painting called 'Woman With A Parasol' painted by Renoir.
I watch red admiral butterflies, dancing among the buddleia.
In the next field behind an old oak tree a fox stares at me,
or is a pheasant in the next field that she's after.
By the yellow Cotswold wall a swathe of wild scarlet poppies, just like a painting by Monet,
but these poppies are all in rows, they remind me of
soldiers marching into battle, and when the winds blows,
their delicate petals fall, it makes me think of all
the young men killed
in wars.
I pick up my paintbrush and paint water cascading over a waterfall,
then a yellow wagtail flies down, searching for insects.
I catch a fleeting glimpse of orange and red goldfish
gliding through the silvery green shimmering water,
darting past as a beautiful dragonfly dips and dives,
in a flash of green and iridescent blue.
Beside the winding path are majestic orange and
yellow sunflowers that would look impressive
in a vase,
but I have managed to capture
their magic like a Dutchman,
called Van Gogh.

Now all I need, is some grey and crimson with raw sienna,
but now it's evening and my painting's finished,
but Mother Nature leaves her best work till last,
she finishes each day, with a firework display.
So all you have to do, is to look around you for
inspiration to paint landscapes, flowers,
or even wildlife, in your garden.
And if I can do it, so can you.

Sandra Wood

Express My Heart

Will these tears in my eyes ever fade?
As my forever love dances away like a fiery parade
A simple 'I love you' turns like a clock to poetry without a clue
A schedule of a life written on paper inscripted with gold
Years, dates and plans turn to words you can express and hold
I gaze out of a clear night sky
As my forever love dances back like coloured moonlight
A simple 'I love you' on a silver glistened sundial fails to turn as though time has stopped all through
Love, happiness and blessed memories all returning by a life turning magical spell,
which causes the innocent, precious heart to once again sing and laugh its graceful note
Love and linger and forever dance like a fiery parade.

Eleanor Darch

Moon Song

I looked into the eyes of the moon
and he smiled,
and said,
go soon
you'll never,
won't ever,
together be
again.

I stood there cold, mind unfolded
to endless whys,
uncertain sighs.
I must go,
I know
whenever
together
can be again.

The moon looked back reflecting thoughts
and winked his eye
when spotlights caught,
so go
you know
if ever
together
is to be.

Sally Plumb

Nothing

I spend time conjuring thoughts of great adventures.
You drop by and I am chastised by your harmonious presence.
Yet I kick back with the tantrums of a child, woe begin the beating of your heart.

The tide is drawing ever nearer and my love is becoming ever deeper.
Sailing you is almost impossible on these dark waters.

If time would wait for me, I would be the first person to rearrange the skies.
But as I fall into slumber,
I recognise what is and what should be.

Alone and quiet, the foundations of my soul harness power and fortitude.
And natural grace is as allusive as it ever was.

What is this 'nothing' that I hunger for?
What is this game that I cannot win?

Amen.

Laura Jane Stanton

Here I Am

Here I am, where are you?
Time to think, lots to do.
Lonely nights, busy day,
Men's work done, a woman's way.
Husband's horror, worried wife,
Loving, hanging onto life.

Feeling love, missing love.
Where's the love from up above?
Struggle hard to see the light,
Bite of cold, fearful sight.
Any love may do today,
Pray the pain will go away.

Kids in khaki, kids so near.
Fears surrounding, hold them dear.
Every day we're one year older,
Feet and hands and hearts grow colder.
Searching deep inside our minds,
For those feelings left behind.

Will you live, will you wait?
Left too early, loved too late.
Turn our hands to stranger things,
Toll the bell, the changes ring.
Will life be the same once more,
When next at our front door, you stand?

Hearts and minds seem strong and certain,
Either side of war's grave curtain,
There you are, here am I
Who will live, who will die?
What is living, where is death?
Both hang on a strangled breath.
Here am I, where are you?

John Jas Jas Smith

The Deserts Of The Night

In the world where,
There are no shadows,
And all has faded into black,
Sounds become magnified,
By the silence of the night,
Where secret lives are concealed,
That will never see the daylight,
We cannot see, but only feel,
The things that give us all a fright,
Imaginations run the freest,
Among the deserts of the night,

For here there exists neither,
Any shape, nor form,
As all give thanks,
For the beginning of each dawn,
And the shades of grey return,
With the light of the rising sun,
To warm the cold that as sent,
Shivers that travel down our spine,
In these darkest of the nights,
As the hands of loved ones,
We hold on to tight.

Pauline Uprichard

Autumn

Wrap your arms around the autumn days.
The colour all around with the chill in the air.
Feelings of the season of the year passing by.
Now when all is asleep – I'm at my best feeling with pride.

Take in the richness of these colours gold and yellows with shades of disappearing green.
Browns and reds with silver glint from the sun which adds the velvet on the leaves falling to the ground . . .

Sweet smells of candyfloss of apples still hanging on the trees, waiting to fall with the swaying of wind or gales that may whistle in our ears.

But the frost is best of all giving me rosy cheeks plus cold hands and feet.
I warm by the fire, with tingling moving up and down my veins till I was warm again.

Take me back to childhood when coal fires burnt bright.
Take me through the long dark evening that awaits.

I toast my bread by the fire with good old farm butter to spread.
There's nothing like it at its best.

Birds sing to you and me, resting on the moss branches singing tunes don't forget me.
With food they like to keep warm and a drink of water to help them on their way.

Hold in tight the autumn days.

M Goodland

Immanuel

We search the hills for shepherds watching their flocks by night,
the air is still, the hillside bare, no angel throng in sight.
We search within the palaces for Wise Men from afar,
but they are counting out the cost and do not heed the star.
Where are you? Shall we know when you come again,
underneath the cardboard box, sheltering from the rain,
single parent trying to cope without food, heat and light,
hidden in darkness, eking out the night;
Prisoner in the arid cell, wherever he may be,
the guilty and the innocent longing to be free;
Father with a crying child, the handicapped and weak,
the old and frail, the ill and poor too proud for help to seek;
The stranger in the townships of Edinburgh and Leeds,
the junkie in the alleyway, who steals to fund his needs;
The rich man in his plenty with things and golden store
who cannot fill the aching void and hungers after more?
We search in vain the mountain top, the sky and stable bare,
the animals they slumber on, the baby is not there.
We find you in the smallest child who is born today.
Help us see, help us to live your life, your Truth, your Way.

Shirley Ann Johnson

Pictures Telling Stories

Art is a form of language
Pictures from one's mind
Telling people stories
They normally could not find.

Putting brush to canvas
Relating to what they see
It's another way of writing
I think you will agree.

Pictures telling stories
Of present and of past
Art showing people's patience
Takes time, can't be completed fast.

Showing people's harmony
In the world in which they live
Expressing feelings not shown in books
Pleasure to the eyes it gives.

Some artists are said to be ingenious
Others thought to be insane
As they put their brush to canvas
They've a message to convey.

Using every detail possible
Their story it is told
Some believe in art's message so deeply
They emboss its frame in gold.

Stephen T Maslen

These Old Rockies

I've always been fascinated by them the beautiful Rocky Mountains of the States.
Just to witness them glistening with fresh snow in wintertime, oh bliss.

As I stand in awe looking at them, my mind wonders what it would be like to scale, conquer these massive objects of sheer wonder.

To me the Rockies epitomise the true spirit of America.

The passion and that power on display, the beauty and strength they show.
As natural as the grizzly bear and mighty eagle.

Those Rockies scrape the US sky.

In summer and winter they shine

For centuries they have displayed a noble presence, showing off their awesome power.

Sadly I'm only wishing, but if I got the chance.
To be all alone with the giant pines and silver streams.

I would be off in a flash, you bet. As long as I had enough food and water, I'd like to stay there forever.
Just me and those Rockies.

USA here I come

Garry Mitchell

Two To One!

When I had finished sleeping
Tears swelled up in my eyes,
As about you I had been thinking
So it came as a big surprise,
I am not one for swearing
Such would not convey my years,
I *still* cannot stop my for you caring
Nor could I eradicate the tears,
I am a being with some feeling
I cannot help to, sometimes, cry,
It sent my senses reeling
When you did lie down to die,
I still love a lot of loving
My loving I do now with others share
I know that you – above in – did for this old one care
What I did find so, so boring
Was your snoring – it hit me pretty deep
It did become so annoying that out of bed
I'd sometimes creep,
But – *still* for you I am caring
I do miss you very much,
I want to be my time with you sharing
But alas you are out of touch,
I am so much still hoping although we be far apart
That I'll soon stop my moping as perhaps
Renewal will still start,
I do still love you deeply
Although you be out of bounds,
Next time that I am sleepy
I'll remember all those sounds,
This old one here has spoken
To bed I must now go
That my heart is broken
I wish for you to know
I'll be coming to join you soon dear
You I do still adore
Although you could be responding I will be fearing
Get rid of that damned snore!

John Leonard Wright

Freedom

I waited for the day to come when I would be set free,
I was like a bird trapped in a cage with nowhere to flap my wings and fly,
Days got longer and each passing sadness filled my heart turning my heart into black
I stayed in my own dark world praying for an angel to set me free
I shouted, cried, screamed and fought but my efforts were in vain.
Instead I smiled, laughed to hide all the pain and sorrow
I was slowly drowning and all hope was lost
I looked up at the sky and wondered if someone was watching over me
I prayed for someone to take these shackles off my feet and let me fly
Deep down I knew this was the end, the end of me
I closed my eyes, took a deep breath and jumped into my own sorrow
As I drowned the pain was agonising and my heart was crushed and shattered into pieces
As I took my last dying breath a white light shone lifting my dying corpse
My heart was on fire with everything dark turning into light
I woke up in paradise with a golden heart, and all my sorrow drowned out of me
I took a step forward, flapped my wings and flew away without looking back.

Esther Wanjiru

The Dark Passenger

Don't get too close
It doesn't bark but bites
Silent in nature but razor sharp in character
Heartless – knows only how to hurt
It hides behind the mask of an innocent
But don't be fooled by its disguise
Its mere existence is unclear but its character is vile and wretched
An unsolicited guest, a parasite
The epitome of malevolent sin
Any trace of light is devoured upon its arrival
Unarmed, no scent or supernatural presence can be perceived
Yet you are conscious of its burden
Interminable . . . you fight to endeavour
But it's futile . . . this creature is clever
No rent is paid; no joy is brought
Just pain and sorrow.
It knows not how to love
Wilder than an animal, no morals or emotions
A monster in every aspect
It cannot be tamed or influenced
Obdurate, ill-mannered and uninvited
One can only pray to God for help
As it feeds only on penance of one's own actions
Any sense of redemption is distant
Only in death will answers be found.
So hence, until ashes remain.
No answers to where this thing came.

Warden Kemadjou Mounga-Njandjo

Untitled

age and sage
on a different page

finer white skin
hair no longer prim

long past her prime
treading time

night-time fears
not with tears

is there an after?
was there a before?

does it matter?
God or nature takes all

the last years pondering
mind still wandering

expecting each day as the last
skeleton frame slowing fast

active thoughts, missing links
backwards leaps for today's chinks

money and goods meaningless
keeps giving them away recklessness

we all have to rescue her from herself
in old age she's lost all meaning and dread

expecting the worst time and again
we begin to wonder if she's sane

One night, tired and sleepy
she mumbles goodnight in her dreams

by next morning she's with us no longer
we'd all known but sadness takes over.

Renate Fekete

When I see you I stare straight past
because I know that if we got back together
we would never last.
Forgetting used to be easy before it was you I was trying to forget.
You said forever and I was stupid enough
to fall for your b******t lies.

Morgan Welsh

The Message In The Bottle

My hands touched yours and you held me tight and fell upon
your knees, with the deep clap of the waves and the rain pouring down.
With one kiss you saved me and kept me at ease.
As I drowned in my tears when you let me go.

You took my heart and carried on your final journey out to sea.
Missing you with every tear, it feels like thunder then lightning;
that strikes the rocks on the coast as the ships sail by, where some don't reach.
I watch with hungry eyes as seagulls fly away into the blue sky.
And sometimes I dive and swim to the shore. Just to call out your name. I feel so free!
With every morning I see the light and stand on distant shores as I look onto the horizon
with fear and worry to the truth that lies beyond.
I have only one question in my heart, 'When will you be back?'
Anxious for any sign of life, I still hear the seagulls dancing above.

I write a message and put it safe into
a bottle then throw it into the ocean for luck.
With time on one silent evening as the tide comes in so close, I return to the shore.
To discover a message inside a bottle beside a rock;
to say that 'the crew is on their way home'.
With joy and laughter, I am so happy to find this message washed up on the sand and
before I go to sleep I sing a love song
under the blanket of stars at night until you reunite with me again.

Nassira Ouadi

Sombre September

It still surrounds the news today
And yet each year, it's like it was yesterday
The desperate pleas and all the fearful cries
All of those lies and another family's heart dies
That sombre September day

All of the questioning and the beckoning
The surrounding sirens were entirely deafening
Lost loved ones and mass despair
The day pain erupted everywhere
On that sombre September day

As the Towers crumbled to the ground
Around the world, hearts began to pound
From this day on, it will never be the same
For now we know who was to blame
That sombre September day.

Serena Dannatt

How The Stories End

Here's a bit of a conundrum
That lately I've been pondering . . . about my childhood friends
Now I'm grown-up
How does *their* story end?

What will the *Munch Bunch* eat when they go out for lunch?
Do they eat their five-a-day . . . friends?
If that's so, there's no one left
And so the story ends.

What happens to *Bananaman* when he's past his sell-by date?
Well of course he inevitably turns black
Ending his days in the compost stack
And there the story ends.

What happens when *Cheep* has chicks and feeds them poor old *Orm*
Sure, he's a meal of nutritious and gourmet grub
But the friendship can't survive
When there is only one left alive
So of course the story ends.

What happens to *Pigeon Street*?
When they've all been shot and put in a pie?
With Molly and Polly now grown and left
I guess it means goodbye
And so the story ends.

What happens when *Danger Mouse* gets left alone in the house?
And the cat is feeling bored?
Best left unsaid how the rodent lost his head
And there the story ends.

Rosie and Jim had a fatal accident
When the barge they lived in capsized at Rickmansworth lock
Although Neil survived he took to the gin
As a result of the trauma and shock
And so the story ends.

The Bucket and Spade lost all its trade
When *Cockleshell Bay* became flooded
Fury drowned and Mr Ship left town
And there the story ends.

Mr Benn is now one-hundred and ten . . . the oldest of all my friends!

The End

Paula Holdstock

Valencia

The cock and the little pig flew to Spain
  in the basket on a balloon
they had lots of wine and a little grain
  and the wind got them there quite soon
the pull was the sun and their lives to gain
  the push, if they stayed, pot next noon.

The flight got them there to Valencia
  where they dined and stayed up quite late
they camped in a park so close to a weir
  and were asked to move on by Kate
'You can't stay here,' she said with a grin
  you could come to my farm,' – a date?

They went with the lass, they'd no other choice
  to the farm on the moors so nigh
they made lots of friends, began to rejoice
  for living with Kate was a high.
The sun they so liked and the pool so moist
  was heaven on Earth by and by.

As time went on they did marry their kind
  the cock to a Rhode Island Red
the little pig grew so big, she did find
  a Gloucester Old Spot very hot. They fed
so well at the banqueting do, a gig
  of the best, then danced till 'twas time for bed.

Robert Shooter

Eyes Like The Sea

She had eyes the colour of the summer sea
And in them a world that was hidden from me
Her skin was as pale as a winter's frost
She always knew what to do but still seemed to be lost.

She had no friends, though everyone knew *her*
Her footsteps were echoed by a whispering whir.
She rarely spoke, though her voice was like a bird's song:
Amazing and mesmerising, though it never lasts for very long.

Her lips always smiled, though her eyes were ever sad
Longing for the comfort that she wanted but never had.
Nobody had known her story; most hadn't cared
But those who wanted to ask were always too scared.

Scared that she was different; she didn't fit in
As beautiful as she was, she could never quite win.
When she was there, she was no more than a background
A one-shoed Cinderella, who had not yet been found.

Although when she was gone she was everybody's interest
they all wanted to know everything, to be interviewed by the press.
The headline was clear, it stood smugly grand:
Teenage girl's body found dead on the sand.

I should have said something, tried to be her friend
I knew that to her I would just be one of them
Inside my head I had been so much better
Although the title penalised me, letter by letter.

A new girl started a week after that day
Her eyes sparkled brightly, a cloudy grey.
She fitted in perfectly, with all the right clothes,
Her make-up was 'correct' and her school bag 'goes'.

With her nobody spoke of girl number one,
Who stayed with me but to the others she was gone.
But in my head she is clear to me,
With her sandy gold hair and her eyes like the sea.

Eve Victoria

Untitled

Carousel of fading dreams. Fading drama. Memories lost.
Free-falling echoes of childhood laughter the wheel of joy turning
faster
faster
then it's over. In an instant. A second. A tick of the clock.
On the carousel of fading dreams. *Great memories are lost.*

Lauren E Cowell

I Am So Glad That He Died For Me

What a great feeling that I should know
Christ The Lord, really loves me
The extent of His love is all around
That He would take my sins to Calvary

I am so glad that He died for me
My eyes can see, my eyes can see
I am so glad that He died for me
He died for a sinner like me.

I am not worthy of His mercy and grace
Although, He chose to give it to me anyway
I have sinned against Him on so many occasions
But He decided to forgive all my sins today.

He suffered for my mistakes on the cross
The nails driven into His hands and feet
I must tell the world of His redeeming grace
Starting with my local town and street.

What an experience to have a special friend
Every time I'm in trouble, he is always near
I do not have to worry about anything
As He will take away all of my trouble and fear.

John Oludotun Showemimo

The Cure

Depression is like drowning,
my body, my mind left lifeless yet my heart still pounding,
you can't breathe, you're choking on survival,
death isn't an option, life is your rival,
you're being dragged down without a fighting chance,
no room for happiness or romance,
just a piece of junk, a waste of air,
no one notices, they don't ever care,
you're just part of the furniture, just something to see,
but they don't look, they see right through me,
I'm a ghost yet my body still breathes,
and then everyone I love gives up and leaves,
who am I and why was I even born?
To become unwanted like a rose thorn,
I'm nothing and that is what I'm worth,
like the birth of child I'm the afterbirth,
I'm unwanted by everyone even me,
I don't know why I'm living I have no reason to be,
and you say I do this all for attention,
that is the opposite I want, I can't stand sensation,
I don't play this act, it isn't something I choose,
it's not something over time I can lose,
I'm sorry, I'm sorry for what you see,
but this is who I am, depression is a part of me,
and maybe one day they will find a cure,
to make me happy so my heart is no longer sore,
until that day comes around,
I will sit and smile and pretend I don't wish my heart wouldn't pound.

Chariti Boland

Depression

I simply cannot explain
What it is like to have
A funeral in my brain

Vitality seeping away from me
My mind and body numb
The blankness of my future
Wishing the undertakers would come

Feeling constantly afraid
But not knowing even why?
Everything is just too much effort
It's an effort to even cry

I just feel nothing
As I slowly, slowly descend
Let this battle be over
I want it all to end

My mind tells me I'm nothing
I don't deserve to live
I'm worthless and useless
I've nothing and nothing to give

'I believe this is the truth'

But the mind's truth lies
And is full of delusional perceptions
I might be onto something here
I might find the answer to this deception

I might go and find some help
That may even help me function
My mind may just be wrong
I may find the answer to my dysfunction

The opposite to depression
Is not everlasting happiness
It's getting out of bed
Making breakfast, answering the phone

Vitality

Niamh Penman

Fearful Of The Future

I'm sat wondering, looking at the stars
Do we have a future? Will it be ours?
Are you the one to share growing old?
Will you be there when I reach out to hold?

Will you share my dreams and hold me tight?
Curl around me when it's cold at night?
Will you still love me as our skin starts to sag?
Or the things you find cute will they start to nag?

I stare at the moon tonight what do I see?
A huge black hole staring back at me.
Dare I reach for the moon and everything bright
or will you vanish out of sight?

My heart is so battered, so bruised and abused
I'm never really loved I've always felt used.
Trust is my issue I beg you to see
Please find the love I have inside me.

The stars are so peaceful they twinkle with hope
Another broken heart, not sure I'd cope
I'll reach for your hand, if you love me take mine
We'll find trust together, we'll grow old, we have time.

Angela Hensley

Them (And The Daughters Of Man Were Fair)

We don't know them but, they know us,
to show themselves would cause a fuss.

There's plenty news for them back here,
watching us all just persevere.

The awful things we often do,
to them we are a human zoo.

The Ten Commandments set in stone,
were not put there for Jews alone.

They were the most religious there,
when they ate lamb for human fare.

Ten was just right computing facts,
from hundreds written from God's pacts.

We could not work data so quick,
they could with snakes who formed a stick.

It may be time for lamb again,
as, sheep get taken from the plain.

Whose table would they sit at now,
Man has adopted golden calves and eats a lot of cow.

Jean Paisley

Through The Looking-Glass

Peering through
To gods and ghouls,
Mythical monsters,
Trans-dimensional fools.
Humanoid machines
With well-laid plans,
On quantum computers
Using Comic Sans.
A consciousness shared -
Between likewise minds,
Sustainable energy
The Tesla kind?
Dimensions unfolded
Once moulded like plaster,
As chaos ensures
An asymmetric disaster,
Entropy wound
And unwound,
Strings, atoms -
Forces – all bound.
Holograph minds,
Still distant and wise,
Deific; non-specific,
An evolutionary ride?
Fizzle or crunch
Or pious-type rapture?
Continue full circle
Or a universal closed chapter?

Craig Aldous

Five Little Angels

One by one they flew their nest
But all we know God takes the best,
My little angels come unto me
And save this world from Man's insanity,
Spread your wings and you take flight
Into the terrors of the night,
Save the souls of those that are lost
By war, famine and flood they have paid their cost,
In some war-torn zone where madness reigns and the devil rules
Seek forth those souls who have obeyed my rules,
For I am the master of my domain
In my house there are many mansions,
For those who change their wicked ways,
Let peace prevail and love begin
And save the world from suffering,
So angels go forth into the world and bring some light into the darkness of their souls,
A beacon of hope I give to you
To light the pathway to my throne.

Jack Iddon

Piggy With A Ponytail

Bertie the pussycat loved to roam
Whenever he could, away from home
One cloudy day it rained so hard
As he walked by an old farmyard

Wet fur he loathed and so he ran
To shelter under the farmer's van
A peculiar noise, 'What's that?' he feared
A squeaking cry so weak and weird

'Twas from the barn that came the sound
He quickly ran inside and found
A piglet hiding in the hay
'Why do you cry, please say?'

'Other piglets laugh, make fun of me
I'm so embarrassed to let you see
Reason I'm feeling sad and frail
Is because I've got a ponytail'

Said Bertie, 'Through the fields we'll walk
We need to have a longer talk
Stay at my house you'll be a pet
So cheer up, no more need to fret'

Plodding on through fields quite wet
All of a sudden Bertie rushed to get
A drink of water from an ancient well
Too hasty was he and in he fell

Piglet hearing the scream was fearful
At the bottom of the well Bertie sat in a puddle
'Please get some help to pull me out'
But Piglet saw no one about

The old well luckily was not too deep
Piglet had an idea, 'Please do not weep
I'll hang my ponytail over the wall
Leap up and grab it, try not to fall'

'That's a brilliant idea you are a star'
To reach it wasn't very far
So up jumped Bertie, grabbed Piglet's tail
Who tugged and pulled, this must not fail

The first attempt and Bertie was out
'You are so clever there is no doubt

Let's head for home not far from here
You'll find a friendly atmosphere'

They sat in the garden for a well-earned rest
When Daddy saw they had a guest
He called for Mother to come quick and see
'A ponytail on a piglet, do you agree?'

'He can't stay here it will not do
The best place for him is in a zoo
He'll grow too big we have no room
I'll contact the zoo this afternoon'

Zookeeper agreed without hesitation
The piglet will be a popular attraction
Immediately arranged for early collection
A pen prepared in a prime location

Unhappy was Piglet to leave his friend
Wondering where his journey would end
Strange animals he'd never seen before
Their welcome calls, could not ignore

Soon he was made to feel at home
A little shelter and space to roam
Ecstatically happy and content was he
From ridicule, laughs and taunts now free

Groomed every day and tail shampooed
Crowds came to see and no one booed
Applaud and admire they could not fail
To love the piggy with a ponytail.

Therese Freaney

World War I – What Is This?

Guns booming, shrapnel flying, rain falling,
Men dying, loved one mourning, death knell tolling,
Winter arriving, snow compacting, soldiers shivering,
Mothers sobbing, children crying, babies whimpering,
What is this?

Gas seeping, men choking, stretchers creaking,
Horses floundering, dugouts relieving, graves opening,
Christmas footballing, enemies smiling, carol singing,
Fighting ceasing, laughter prevailing, handshaking,
What is this?

Operations resuming, watches timing, whistles blowing,
Guns blasting, noise deafening, over-the-top climbing,
Snipers hiding, craters opening, bodies welcoming,
Men drowning, rescuers appearing, men shouting,
What is this?

Tanks rolling, men crumpling, casualties increasing,
Aeroplanes flying, bullet ricocheting, buildings collapsing,
Pilots braving, planes crashing, hospitals awaiting,
Soldiers decreasing, men volunteering, weddings rushing,
What is this?

Sun shining, heat sweltering, unwashed skin itching,
Boots squelching, hair matting, mud clinging,
Sores rubbing, fleas biting, wounds bleeding,
Food rationing, rats running, letters arriving,
What is this?

Bicycle wheels turning, messenger alighting, telegram delivering,
Women shrieking, wives fainting, families grieving,
Cemeteries crowding, headstones shining, names engraving,
Flowers blooming, roses scenting, bees humming,
What is this?

Zeppelins droning, civilians crouching, bombs dropping,
Earth shattering, explosions terrifying, panic striking,
Dawn breaking, carnage unfolding, firemen searching,
Ambulances saving, doctors tending, nurses comforting.
What is this?

Men's spirits reviving, hearts mending, memories lingering,
Poppies growing, wounds healing, soldiers returning,
People rejoicing, not forgetting, prayers ascending,
Cenotaph rearing, bugles blowing, medals glistening,

What is this?

Papers signing, generals saluting, bigwigs leaving,
Church bells ringing, choirs singing, flags flying,
Wreaths laying, veterans marching, hands clapping,
Bands playing, emotions surging, tears falling,
What is this?
War is this!

Irene Greenall

Untitled

A silent night,
Not a sound to be heard
Not the hooting of an owl, nor the chirping of a cricket,
Not the flutter of a bird, nor the howling of a wolf,
Not the beat of a heart, not a breather in sight,
Side by side, ebony boxes emerge,
Held together by Cupid's grasp,
As descent begins,
And the earth covers what once was,
A silent night, not a sound to be heard but the whistling of the wind,
As it whisks lost lovers' souls beyond the cusp of reality.

Btisem Derfoufi

The Old Mill

By the side of a stream,
In the lee of a hill,
Stands Johnny Holdsworth's old Victorian mill,
Now all quiet, empty and still.

All the machinery long since gone,
Sold to scrap merchants,
Or out to Hong Kong.
No longer the sound of the loom's mad pound,
The hot wheels turning as the belts fly round.
All well tuned and finely set,
Weaving Johnny Holdsworth's top quality moquette.

A relic of the Industrial Revolution,
Creating wealth but causing pollution,
No longer its chimney, belching smoke,
No boiler fire to light or stoke.
It stands like a monument to days long past,
Built by Victorians and made to last.

Holdsworth's moquette had worldwide fame,
If you journeyed around by bus or by train,
Or even flew in an aeroplane.
You could rest assured that the seat you did sit on,
Would have been covered with Holdsworth's pattern.

It took all of the crafts and all of the skill,
Employed within Johnny Holdsworth's old mill,
Down by the stream in the lee of a hill,
Now all quiet, empty and still.

Keith Empsall E Holmes

We Reap What We Sow

This world can be good and it can be evil
It is up to us who we choose to trust
Whether we win or lose
For God helps those of us who help themselves
Should it be love or lust
Because the Lord is looking from above

We need to teach the children from the start
Otherwise they can end up with a broken heart
So I recommend we all start to get smart
As we reap what we sow
As you already know.

Sally Fovargue

There Is A Grave I Know

There is a grave I know,
Whose headstone bears the names
Of those I loved so long ago.

I knew them then as quick,
Opinionated in their views,
With arguments of conviction and attitude.

Affection and advice they gave,
And willingness to help,
Standing in imperfection of self.

They are silent now, unhurried,
Yet still they come to me
In mixed up fantasies of dreams.

They never try and keep me
With them there, knowing that my
Time will come with them to share.

Yet there is nothing in their
Condition laid, that makes me want
To lie with them the same.

Robert W Lockett

The Week Before The Deed

She lay in darkness,
Heart slowed to a still,
Lungs once pistons,
Last breath to fill

Mind once lucid,
Sharpness and clear,
Sliced into pieces,
By time's brutal spear

Her old greying fingers,
Clutching my hand,
I shared the memories,
Now alien land

What do I witness,
Creation destroyed,
A hollowed out husk,
Once full of our joys

So goodbye sweet girl,
From times years ago,
My bruises won't fade,
Never to yellow

So Sunday's the day,
That we scatter your shell,
Spread on the beach,
That you once knew so well.

Matthew Roberts

The Underground #2

Not in your system, but the drainage system, yes sewers are where many people live,
In colourful rags, potions, insanity, syringes, some HIV, hepatitis C or B, the plague,
There is a world in parallel *Camera Obscura* to flat metronome beating one of yours.

You, clean shirt and tie, smart skirt and jacket find them odious or are just oblivious,
That was another cruise to the office or dropping off the children before the meeting,
The aroma of suburbia was becoming a little tainted, well, quite unpleasant she said.

There was a wilt in the air yet it was high summer, so someone said perhaps speak,
The rose bushes were in decline, the manicured lawns were not quite so neat, nasty,
Yes, it was all a little too much, but then people in rags screaming: 'the end is near'.

But do not carry a Bible their eyes ablaze with the fire of an inferno: end, what end?
Then the sanity sanitation teams entered the underground, psychiatrists and police,
Underground people have different words, expressions: 'shrinks', 'pigs' or 'Babylon'.

Everything and everyone are clean again, but the labyrinth causes land subsidence,
Your home is at risk; your society faces collapse, wipe away your tears and go down
In the underground and meet your destiny because here death is random like a dice.

Nigel Pearce

Mother Golightly's Lament

Go lightly to war my sons, on battle my sons were bent.
Go lightly into war my sons and lightly they were sent.
Lightly through fields of poppies, lightly off they went.

Seven sons had I, seven of the best.
Lots were drawn and my seven were sent, along with all the rest.
My eldest off to France he went, to battle in the Somme.
He and his brother fought bravely together
but sadly not for long.

Then came my twins, the trouble two! Together they were from birth.
Off to separate battles they went, singing and full of mirth.
Who knows what horrors my young ones saw?
Or how they quit this Earth.

The other three were close in age and each I loved in turn.
Some were killed in battle, their country's honour earned.
All my sons and all were killed, the fates of some I never learned.

The letters came in endless floods, the postman I did spurn!
When they were read, for each one I wept and sorrowfully did burn.
All hope was gone, all hope except for one.
My youngest lad, my pretty one for whom I prayed for long.

I prayed to God to keep him safe and return to me just one.
Just one I prayed of my seven sons, for all the rest are gone.
But there is no God when it comes to war!
No one can answer my prayers.

The last of my seven sons took the war.
Now my life is lonely and bare.
Some of the seven were buried in state with colours and bugles played.
Some became 'unknown soldiers', just pieces of arms and legs.
Buried together with their comrades I found out at a later date.

The others lie rotten in an unmarked grave, the poppies of France know their fates.
I hope death did not trick them and force them long to wait.
I pray to God they all went quickly and made it to Heaven's gates.

Seven sons had I and all seven were sent to a foreign country to die.
Go lightly to war young men, for lightly you are sent.
Go lightly into war my sons, if on serving your country you're bent.
Take care my lads and be wary, heed your mother's lament
For if lightly into war you go, at leisure you will repent!

Fiona Crosby

A Candle's Glow

Whenever I light a candle now
It will mean much more you see
A memory will stir in my mind
Of gallant men who died for me.

A hundred years ago a war started
Filling the nation with dread
These candles are there to remind us
Of the many souls now dead.

Young in heart you were
The cream of our land
Eager to defend and fight for us
For our freedom you did demand.

You rest there in foreign soil
Nothing can harm you now
Know that you're in a billion thoughts
You're being remembered here and now.

For candles are burning all over the land
In our thoughts you are with us yet
The lights are here in your memory
But . . . 'We never will forget.'

Winnie Milnes

Yesterday And Tomorrow

Yesterday and tomorrow
Make it mine
Time has run out
In the evening of our life

Yesterday and tomorrow
Death a fellow traveller
On the road to hell
Pell mell, selling seashells

Yesterday and tomorrow
Could be who knows!
Will you be my beau
Hold my hand – yesterday or tomorrow.

S M Thompson

The Bubble In My Mind

As the iridescent light gets refracted, my thoughts become increasingly distracted.
The light bounces off the edges of the bubble, it's blinding like the light at the end of a tunnel.
The bubble floats effortlessly through the sky, and into my mind's eye.
I escape the mundane, as my thoughts are placed on a higher plane.
Problems evaporate in the bubble, as there is no worldly trouble.
All that can be felt is peace and love and harmony, if this was in the real world it would be sold commercially.
This is how I escape the shackles, of what life wants me to tackle.
Drift, float, glide, enjoy the carefree existence in this place where I come to hide.
No harm can come to me here, I live with abstinence from fear.
This is the bubble in my mind, where my inner peace is perfectly aligned.

James Lloyd

Put Your Hope In Me

As you sit and ponder and find that you have no hope,
Then look up and place your hope in Him.

I remember rejoicing with the Angels
As I watched you being created.
Long before you were ever a thought
in your parents' minds
I had laid out a plan for your life.
When I crooned over you inside your
Mother's womb, it was me who sang the
soft lullaby of promising you then, that I
would always be with you.

My Dearest Child, I long so much for you
to turn to Me and place your heart in my hand.
I have such blessings in store for you, that all Heaven waits
in anticipation for you to receive them.
Yet I cannot force them upon you my Child.
You must reach out and trust in Me
and I will never let you down.
When hope has left you and you are all alone,
that is when my Hope will touch you and set you free.

What is your Hope Lord I hear you ask
that differs so much from mine?
Ah, the difference is my Child, My Hope lies
within you waiting for the time
that He can spring up and lift you beyond all understanding.
Then my Hope will set you free once again, to hear my voice,
to lift your eyes and see beyond the darkness that surrounds you.
Then you will come to Me and I will sing once
more again the lullaby of old.
That I will always be with you no matter
what the future holds.

Come my Child you are the apple of my eye.
I dance and sing over you.
Come my Child and trust in Me
and walk in the plans I have for thee . . .

Elizabeth Jane Bastow

On Remembering A Picture

It was a picture
I remember it now
A picture of a man holding a lantern
And I remember how he spoke to me without speaking
I thought that was rather strange
But I liked him though
And I knew
Somehow
He liked me
Someone said to my young curiosity
It is called The Light of the World
And I wondered then
How could such a small lantern light all the world
Someone said
The picture is out of date
And I wondered
How could light be out of date
But I liked him though
That man who chose to wait
With unending patience
Wait
In the golden light of his lantern
What was he trying to say
what was he waiting for
That man
Who spoke without speaking to the lad that I was
That man
Who stood with his light shining
Bright
As the sun.

John Jones

Gone But Not Forgotten

Rain falls
Let's play inside
Dressing up box, child's play
The theatre of forever
Lost days.

David Archibald

My Angel

My angel,
She's always watching.
She is always there.
She wipes away the tears that I cry,
And holds me close until they stop.
She fights my battles for me,
Even when I'm in the wrong.
She chases away the fears that haunt me,
And loves me with all her soul.
My angel,
Always watching.
She is always there to catch me if I fall.
That constant safety net,
Her gentle guiding hand.
She'd face down anything to protect me,
And she has a heart of pure gold.
The people that know her don't realise how lucky they are,
She goes to the ends of the earth for everyone she loves.
Friends, family and sometimes complete strangers,
Because that's how selfless she is.
They're still not as lucky as me though,
Because God gave me an angel,
To watch over and protect me.
To listen to my worries and fears,
To console me in my darkest days.
My angel,
Always watching,
Always caring.
Because God gave her to me.

Natassia Cole

I Think . . .

You affixed your glare upon me,
But I, only a glance,
In those deep brown eyes,
Shone three words,
'I love you'.

I hug you -
Even give you a kiss, or two,
I am not that much of a fool, am I?
I only do it for you.

Though inside it burns,
A thousand fires,
I quickly glance back -
Then away again.

Hide emotions hide,
But my foolish heart,
Falls once again into a pit of sinful shame,
As I internally burn, without a screech of pain.

Ever since I lay beside you,
With your arms wrapped around my fragile waist,
Enclosing on me as if I was easy prey,
Trapped and fearful,
I could not escape.

I am your keeper but seek no desire,
I am only a baby, a young child,
Craving for the love I surely need -
Don't I?

I don't like it,
I don't feel comfortable,
This is not right,
But my glass heart bleeds for more.

I am unstable,
Can you not see?

A teenage girl, without a dream,
You are my keeper and I am just a fool,
But my heart, brain, soul are too weak.

I love -
I think . . .

Jessica Smith

Little Tree

This little tree stands alone I see
So straight and proud of its destiny
Home to birds and squirrels and such
From this life it does not ask much

Just water to drink and the sun to warm
Protecting the critters from the heat and the storm
It gives us our air and takes away the waste
Provides us with beautiful fruits to taste

But its family is dying through over deforestation
We have to find a way to help this situation
Look after the trees for without them we die
All will be lost, earth, sea and sky

So take time to think about the trees that you see
For without them there would be no you or me
They work so hard to keep the earth healthy
And are being destroyed to make people wealthy

Let's help this little tree's family now
It really does not take much know-how
If everyone would plant a tree
Alone no more would little tree be.

Anne Craig

Spring

As she lay
on her knees
surrounded by these brown-coloured leaves
she gazed up high
so high
it was like she
was floating above
the sky
but a cold breeze
soon sent
shivers down her spine
shaking it off
she picks up
a dandelion
she made her wish and threw it
sending it flying in the wind
the birds whistling in sync
she starts to sing
you see
it's not autumn anymore
it's spring
no more autumn leaves
just a warm summer breeze.

Jamie Walker

Sunshine

Where's the sunshine
Don't be late
Everyone looks forward
the sunshine is great

Lotion on
Burning tense
Cover their heads
Cap makes sense

Sadness goes
When the sun comes out
To the beach
Children scream and shout

Children play in the waves
Bucket and spade to hand
Sunshine falls
Digging holes in the sand

Pebble throwing
Shells collecting
Mother looks on
Child swimming

Crab catching
Rock climbing too
Pools of water
Sun still shining through.

Darren Bly

Fisherman's Dream

Whilst picking twigs and berries
O my old train heart
Pulled full steam ahead
To see a girl so pretty
With strands of golden hair
Drifting teasingly downstairs, downstream
Please don't wake my aching limbs
Should this be but a dream

She stopped upon a riverbank
Uncoiling and change of shape
To a silvery fish so plum
Must save this angel
Place her where she belongs
So I raced upon the land
Only to wake in dead of night
With fishing rod in hand.

Rodger Moir

Dad, Mum

I am awake.
I am sleeping.
I am dreaming
Your hand on my shoulder.
You came to me.
This you start to unfold.
Safe within the knowledge of your spirit
You came to me with unconditional love.
Dad, Mum
You'll always be by my side.
With your spirit within me
My life will go on.
I love you
Dad, Mum
Your spirit is within me to go on.

Julie May Wiles

Memory Of Gym

My eyes are burning, tears are running
Body is aching, telling of pain
Tissues were finished, nothing to wipe with
Mind is saying more pain to gain

He is twitching, to show his muscle
She is running with weights on hand
He is shouting don't stop, do more
She is crying with pleasure of pain

He is yelling you are strong, do more
She wants to scream, but who would listen
Music is loud and the floor is lively
Movers are abound with the rhythms of dance

Sweat is mixing in the air with dampness
The odour is spreading, hard to breathe around
Anxious minds looking at the ticking clock
Is my time yet? May that question haunt my mind.

Bindu Johny

The Drummer

In legend he strides along misty hillsides,
Heroic silhouette against flying clouds,
In dreams we hear his drum a-blazing
Far across the noise of the battlefield.
He marches down the strife-torn centuries,
Ahead of his brave battalion, drumsticks a blur,
Beating time for brave hearts to follow,
Stout boots to move, standard held high.
Drummer Rigby will join the ranks of the fallen,
March with the drummers of centuries past,
Not killed in the heat of battle, for all his courage,
But hacked down cruelly on an English street.
And soldiers, wherever they are, will raise a glass
And toast from their hearts 'Here's to you,
Drummer Rigby, and all the brave drummers
We have known, here's to you, fierce brave comrades,
We will remember you till our lives are done.'

Liz Davies

Husband, Brother, Son

The same brown eyes and rugged jaw
Hair now shorter than before
Suntanned face and laughter lines
Ever handsome, this man of mine.

Shoulders broad and chest so toned
Upper arms finely honed
Muscular hands, fingers long
Where my own hands always belong.

Abdomen bronzed, flat and taut
Exercised well as you've trained and fought
Legs still strong though battle-scarred
Tired feet have worked too hard.

The same man who came home at last
Rockets and missiles a thing of the past
A final medal and goodbye to friends
This particular war now at an end.

So why, as I look where you lie, now at peace
Did the guns in your mind and thoughts never cease?
So why, after so many years
Could you not control the panic, the fear?

Deep down I think I always knew
One day my fate would be losing you.
A man's body can take any amount of pain
Patched up and fixed again and again.

But his mind can be shattered, harder to repair
Plummeting down to the depths of despair
The public face hiding deep-seated scars
Memories locked in, feelings debarred.

Released at last from unspeakable woe
The battle is over with your ultimate foe
I understand now the code you lived by
You took your life and I know why.

Dena Richards

The Bluebells On A Dorset Down

They grow all over this Dorset down,
With birch trees every way,
Where you can walk and lose your frown,
And know, such peace all day;
If you come here when you are free,
From south or east or west,
Or just below the Irish sea,
It's here – you'll find the best;
It is a place that's hardly known,
Except who live this way,
Yet, here you can wander on your own,
Or with friends to make the day;
That's why all those who soon complain,
And often are depressed,
Who come here full of hurt and pain,
Can get things off their chests;

For soon you'll find you're in a field,
Where bluebells have their say,
With every element that's sealed,
As you go round each way;
Where bluebells spread out like a sea,
As you walk round each wood,
So you might change and choose to be,
The kind of man you should;
For here you walk for miles and miles,
And wade up to the knee,
Round coppices, and gates and stiles,
As far as you can see;
And soon you'll find you no more care,
What critics have to say,
As no more blind you stand and stare,
At what you've seen all day;

But if you're one who has come here,
To ponder every leaf,
With blackbirds singing in your ear,
Yet still have no belief;
And here you wander in the blue,
Round every path in sight,
And He is no more real than you,
Your mind needs putting right;
For in springtime of the year,

In the sedateness of this wood,
If you take in every wonder here,
And meditate as you should;
Here is a sapphire on the land,
A jewel in every way,
That's meant to help you understand,
How God has had his say . . .

Tom Ritchie

Henna Night

The moon dressed supramundane,
Accompanied by the stars
Lit up the sky at that night.
The roof boasting in glamour,
A majestic crown of ruby, emerald and diamond lights.
Family, friends and neighbours establish around,
Air filled with cheer and laughter.
An amateur beats the Dholki drum
Singing folk songs
A few wailing gibberish out of tune.
The friends tie a bracelet on the bride-to-be,
Dangling down the wrist,
Consists of brightly coloured pompoms
Threaded dried fruit and shelled nuts,
A symbol of their friendship.
Henna painted on their hands and feet,
Flowery patterns using matchsticks.
Nibbles of sweet are hand fed,
The elders, some stroke her cheeks, others her head,
Blessing her happiness and tranquillity,
The ceremony comes to an end.

Shazia Kausar

A Childhood Dream

You were a beautiful Hackney pony for all to see
You always did your best for me.
You were my friend for so many years
You were there through all my laughter and tears.

Dear Danny Boy you were my best friend
You came when I needed my sadness to mend.
My daughter had died and broken my heart
You were there for me along with your cart.

Children were excited to ride with us
Then out they would jump and give you a fuss.
You pulled the carriage with such great pride
When taking from church the groom and the bride.

How strong you could be we were often shown
You gave all the rides with never a moan.
Up hills you pulled with all your might
The carriage was heavy but you never took flight.

How elegantly you marched with a pipe band
How proudly you stood when I asked you to stand
Photos were taken, how grand you looked
For other events we were often booked.

For fun out on a drive we would often go
Just down to the shops we were caught in the snow.
We'd take friends to the sea shore to buy ice cream
To have a high-stepping Hackney was my childhood dream.

Danny Boy how did you make so many dreams come true
You put smiles on the faces of all whom you knew.
Dreams do come true as I was shown
If I hadn't met you I would never have known.

Gail Newman

They Do Not Hear Me

Lost in the complexity of mind
Floating aimlessly, going nowhere
More I try to get out of the sand,
More I feel sinking, deep fear.

Whatever I grasp to stop from sinking
Found to be hopeless, I ask why?
I can hear their laughs and jokes
But they don't hear me. Should I die?

The day I came, remember very well
My parents left me here, queries why?
Didn't know then, know not now
In my mind I feel very lonely.

I was left in a home for the retarded child
They do not hear me and I ask why?
Soft and tender feeling for my mother
Brings sharp pains and I bleed quietly.

'Mentally challenged', sensitively defined –
What is the parameter? I ask in my mind.
Why am I here and not with my mother?
Where is my father? They do not hear.

Somen Sen

Racial Burning

The Lord's cross burns, the flames ignite the night,
Terrified eyes watch, a hell-on-earth sight,
No religion, no hope, no mercy, no god,
The ashes fall, where these victims previously trod,
The victims, they weep, and circle in despair,
Smell of burnt wood soaked up in their hair,
Only a few left, many limp in a sack,
Cold faces lifeless, cold, blank, black.

Jay Shellito

The World Situation

I daren't foretell what this will be.
According to Bible students
The present system will collapse
But a new Paradise Earth will result.

Is this the end of another civilisation?
Such as has happened in history?
Who are to be the chosen few
And preserved?

If wars get any worse
There'll be nobody left.

Keith Murdoch

I Hunger

I vow to you; we'll be there one day,
When the dusk cascades into craving dredge,
And the porcelain oyster shells slurping down our throats,
Let us laugh at the jazz dancers, kaleidoscoping his hand in that shifting manner,
Let us laugh
Let us be there one day.

One day,
Muttering the bustle of crosiers and timber,
At the checked marble bar, the women come and go,
Men dance to dizziness of purity,
And some raise their brows, like question marks
To such.

We'll be there.
Of cranks from gears, and crinkles of leather;
Let us dance.
Dance with them;
To lead into abacinate love; burning our coals for eyes.
Yet, you'll question the moon's stay,
'It's too late, let's go home,' you say.
Don't
Please.
Let us be there.

As roads coil each other in sultry wars of territories,
The birds chirp to the harmonic blues;
Men are clouded in smouldering cigars
And the children gaze from their storey windows,
Hands supporting their faces,
Dreaming.
Of that one desire.
Just as I did.

Just as I do.

Kimberley Regan

Wet, Wet, Wet

When flood waters gain
a foothold
rains must bring despair.
One can't sit beside the
fire's glow.
In the wet wet wet wet wet
of a scarce wet salt sea air
of't a damp coarse horse hair
lair
And so to sit soaked in a
comfy old armchair
And in thy guts mouth to
munch a soggy sandwich brunch
a soak'ed lunch shop's fair.
Now sitting alone in the dark only
muddy tides remain. No joke
in the wet wet wet wet wet too
remember Noah and his ark
in the wet wet wet wet wet it's
politics you bet, no lark.

Robert Collins

Mixed Emotions

You tell me you love me but I'm not enough
You tell me you want me but this life is too tough
I wish you were here but you're too far away
I wait and wait for you every day

I'm so angry and broken, jealous and in love
It's as if you were something sent from above
You make me happy and sad, even at the same time
You can murder me in seconds without it being a crime

So if all of this love is true and real
Why is there anything more to feel?
If what we have is something pure
Why would you want someone else to adore?

You cannot love two people at a time
It would not be fair and it would not be fine
I'd tell you to stay or you can leave with her
But how could I say such horrible words?

I don't want you to go, please don't misunderstand
I'm just fighting each feeling that's coming to hand
It's raining outside and it's raining in me
Now I'm sharing my thoughts for the whole world to see

It's as if I'm going 'round in circles constantly
I break and get up to put it bluntly
It's the falling that kills me time after time
So if I'm already dead, what's next in line?

Explain to me what this is that I'm feeling
Tell me when it's safe for me to start healing
What happened between us, we never planned
So explain this moment because I don't understand.

Georgia Head

Alice's Eyes

Blue tears cry
Draining fluid from your corneas
No longer sparkling
Just pearl white
With black pools, blinded fright
Hands cover your dreary face
Open windows, so your eyes can't get misplaced
Hair which was once golden now is weary, fine as lace
Your body has fallen, your tongue no longer can taste
Your voice has been stolen and contaminated
Your ears can no longer hear the words you long to feel
Searching for the answers buried within your palms
Trying to follow the lifeline
Maybe someone will come and rescue you if you found the end
This room has become your resting womb
Too scared to move, to grow up and deal with winter's cold cocoon
Seeking comfort in the fairy-tale stories
Not believing that where you are laid are cobweb fantasies
Poisoned with manipulative enemies
You long to seek the outside life
Let your eyes breathe colour and light
But you've become a mannequin for everyone's delight
To use and abuse, torment
To dress their lives with amusement
You've dug in too deep in the merry-go-round pages
So you take the dirty mirror of rejection
And think that any attention must mean love and affection
Epic minutes in disorientation
Fingertips brushing your blistered lips
Sitting in your corner of illumination
People clouding your silenced thoughts
Your body becomes bleached with everyone's haunts
Only your eyes witness the truth in these taunts
Stitched and sewn together with harlequin nightmares
Scarred forever from the chains
You close your eyes to hide the pain

Kiss the book titles where you escape
If only your eyes could speak for your lonely heart
Unlock the padlock where people keep you on guard
You'll be set free from your demons
To finally see the sun rise.

Emily Ryder

No More Secrets

Can you ever see,
What you are doing to me?
You are this, you are that,
One minute you are the cat:
Purring, loving, so sincere.
The next, my goodness!
You are the scorpion!
The sting in your tail tells all
Those secrets I pick up on.
Do not let anyone
Be bad to you.
You will conquer and come through.
Feel, think, be strong again.
Do not let anyone rain on your parade.
You see, I've seen your pain
Again and again.
Dedicated to my daughter
An inspiration. The scorpion
In my life.
Sweet, sincere
And oh so dear to me.

Wendy Deaves

Summer Holidays

The sun was shining through the trees,
The sky so blue.
It's the summer holidays,
So much for the children to do.
Riding their bikes, skateboarding too.
Go to the beach with a bucket and spade,
Go crabbing too.
There will be fun and laughter all around,
We won't want the summer holidays to ever end.

Anita C Walker

Bags And Boxes

Bags on top of bags
Boxes on top of boxes
Homelessness decry
Loss of belongings awry
Forced to live apart from her son
By a narcissist who knows not
Or is aware of what deeds he has done.
The words of hurt
That caused her falls
For self-pity she did not cry
But was brave
Because no one heard her cries
No one listened, no one heard
But suffer to the end
She watched as those around her
Crumbled one by one
Pity them now
They do not know
Forgive them as they know not
What they have done
The pain they caused
Soldiering on in no-man's-land
No goal, no aim, no joy
Just stillness
Misunderstood because they do not
Understand
The aloneness I suffer
Not to be part of them
Is to destruct and to self-harm
As is to be part of them too.

Her beauty fades day by day
But still remains to those who can see
Her life is about the lives who have died
Who soldiered on as brave as she
She remains today as she always did –
Yesterday was her day
Which remains
Movement hurts

Muscles clam
Breaks away
Calms her down
As she can pretend she is still there
With her son in her arms on the beach
Wishing she was there again
And nothing had moved on.

Patricia Aubrey

Chastity

Nothing.
That is all I see.
All I can hear.
Everything is fuzzy.
There are lights in front of me.
Blue and red.
I feel sick.
I was doing the right thing. I think.
I told him no.
I told him I was not ready for this.
The slam of the door as the tears touched my eyes.
I just didn't want it.
Now he is lying there, in his crushed car.
He is dripping with death, outside my door.
He sped his car, crashed not far.
He died.
All because I said no to the sin.

Connor Empringham-Green

In The Shadows

Every morning she comes to this part of the pier
Just as the sun begins to rise
She stares out at the sea
The sun reflects off the water
The light catches the waves and sparkles
Like thousands of diamonds on the surface
She catches her breath breathing in its saltiness
Closing her eyes she listens to the crescendo of the waves
Crashing against the shore and lets out a sigh
Her blue eyes scan the horizon
A seagull lets out a loud cry
Swooping down onto the sandy beach
Looking for its breakfast
She bows her head and whispers quietly
Her eyes full of tears she turns and walks away
I watch her every day and hear her prayers
As she remembers the day she lost her loved one
When he drowned many years ago
Trying to save a child who had swum too far out
She lived but he did not
A hero he would always be remembered
Her companion, her life and her heart
She would always remember him
I am her comforter, the healer of her wounds
I will never leave her, always will I stay.

Diane Mills

Thieves

Do they come at dead of night?
Do they not like their sleep like us?
Maybe the urge to rob and steal
Can be explained by every cuss!

Envy, poverty, greed, lack of respect
Quick fix to a problem of debt
Reasons or excuse to help themselves
To whatever they can get.

Perceive we this as *Nature's* way?
In-built instinct to survive
Moral duty abandoned
Their families too must live.

Was it trusted visitors?
Who made themselves much at home
Light-fingered with a friend's cash.
Could they for this atone?

Mostly personal experience
Has not been of human sin
Like that roving pussycat
We should never have let in.

'Twas our hard-won rabbit leg
(Not easy to buy off the peg)
That tabby plundered within
To devour in secret whim.

Or the cheeky squirrel's dash
To pick up jewelled objects.
Or was it the thieving magpie
Burying a ring in its nest?

A hungry stray old terrier
Hovering outside our gate
Owned once by a bad carer
Kicked out on night street, late.

Should we deny it shelter
Or a drink, or a food plate?
Is this the human answer
To bear another's burden?

But one night, *someone* came inside
Who stole our cherished things.

In human rage we have out-cried
'Hope someone his neck wrings!'
(Kinder second thoughts prevail –
There's always the insurance!)

Much better still, our thoughts to leaven,
Make sure our treasure is in heaven!

Jo Allen

What A Sweet Sound

(In Memory Of Katharine Hannah, 1974-2014)

What a sweet sound
The dawn chorus
Man could not wake up to a more beautiful thing
Than the trills of the birds in the trees
On the rooftops
Far and near
Duets and solos as the breeze rustles leaves
Branches dancing
Morning has truly come for all
God has decorated the Earth with radiance and love.

Katharine Hannah

Mystical Island

The water shimmers gently in the evening light
As I gaze across to that far-off distant shore
And I wonder what is on that mystical island
That compels me to stand here and stare in awe

There's no boat or bridge to reach onto the island
Too far for me to swim the treacherous water deep
But is that island the place, that will fulfil my dreams
Could it be there, my eyes will no more sadly weep?

The utopia I've searched for all my life's eluded me
Each castle that I've built tumbled and fell
As the mortar that is life decays through lack of faith
Pushing me ever deeper into this private hell

So maybe mystical island it's on you, there is the key
And happiness for me starts on your shore
Tragedies and failures, shattered dreams, idealistic plans
Will be forgotten, as I walk through Heaven's door.

He dove into the water.

Don Woods

The Night Wind

In meditative mood, I paused a while;
The sea-foam murmured on the muted sands;
The stars blazed in the velvet blue; the moon
Hung full, serene: the night wind whispered low.

In diamond sparks athwart the moonbeam's track
The ripples broke. Upon the wrinkled beach
I lay in silent wonder, the sea grass
All around me: the night wind whispered low.

This peace denied what memory recalled –
An enemy's force, his cruelty and power
Spreading an evil gospel through the world.
It cannot be: the night wind whispered low.

Yet, in more distant lands, above the cries
Of homeless women, children without food.
Above the makeshift homes of rootless folk
Whose crops have failed, the night wind whispered low.

And so the night grew cold, the stars shone down
Malignantly. The air was chill; the foam
Thundered upon the booming, echoing sands.
I shivered while the night wind howled in glee.

Caroline Buddery

The Greatest Lesson

Where were you when I was young
Weren't you supposed to be there
You didn't protect me or make me feel safe

What were you doing, I was just a child
I could not understand why you did not come home
No one would answer me straight

I did not feel too bad because
I thought you would come back one day
He is happy now, they said

So why were they all so sad
My mum couldn't speak, just cried
I did not understand

I saw you the next morning you know
Standing outside the window all dressed in white
A man stood beside you with his hand upon your shoulder

And then you were gone . . .

Years later I know you died helping a friend at work
Seven thousand volts was your reward that night
Five hours of struggling to stay on this Earth

Nothing they could do . . .

So I forgive you for not being there to protect me
For not making me feel safe
For not teaching me to fish or fix cars

You helped a friend in need that night
The greatest lesson I could ever learn
Thank you Dad . . .

George Dellipiani

Emotional Tides

Water:
Fluid magic,
The strongest element,
From gentle wave to raging sea
It flows;
Never still and never silent,
Surging round obstacles
Onwards through time;
Tides turn . . .

And so:
The human heart,
Sea-stirred, has moods that ebb
And flow, in stillness or frenzy,
Restless . . .
Until they come to journey's end,
That love that nurtures true,
To rest a while,
Becalmed.

Lynne Emmerson

First Love

He could not remember
your name.

While I remembered
your birthday . . . your lips.
Your fragrance.
And you who cast me aside
as if I were old clothes
to the rag and bone man . . .
upon his horse and cart.

Yes, I . . . who still dreams
sweet and upon corners . . .
snow and blizzards at the park.
Sharing our last cigarette,
walking to Seaton Carew
to see the spring tide.

Making love in long grass,
sharing our dreams . . . which died.
Losing all I held sacred,
though a fool of youth,
trembling . . . hands shaking,
tears unable to hide,
for I loved you even more
at our last goodbye.

Norman Dickson

Dirty Tricks

The moths of my mind are working overtime.
There is a big hole in my trust for you.
You were working in Rome,
I was left at home.

I decided to visit my best friend.
I rang her doorbell, no reply.
A rain cloud burst and opened up the sky.

It had started to rain.
They came into view, running and laughing,
Soaked to the skin.
She didn't see me, she only had eyes for him.

You said you were working in Rome.
Why didn't you tell me?
Oh why didn't you tell me
You were playing dirty at home.

Sylvia Papier

The Bugle Calls

Tears can't mend
A heartbreak
Only memories ease the pain
But things can
Never be the same
1914-18 came
How could the world
Stay the same?
One second a child
Next a soldier
How do you cope?
Just pray and hope
Memories are there
In that
Long, long trail of winding
From darkness
From sorrow
Will come a new tomorrow
Another day
A new beginning.

Margaret Parnell

The Astronomer's Mistress

The black velvet lawn of sky is daisied over with stars.
I have picked the brightest, woven a sparkling chaplet
To place upon your brow.
I have fashioned a pendant from moonbeams
To hang between your breasts.
I have plucked an eye from Cetus
To set and glint in your navel.
I have woven cloth of gold from sunshine
To gird your hips.
From errant strands of the Hair of Berenice
I have twisted forget-me-knots
To tie at your wrists
And round your ankles
I shall fix bells made from starlight
To chime when you dance.
I have wrought a cloak
From the silver lining of a storm cloud
To keep the stardust off your shoulders
All I need now is you.

Alexander Hamilton

You Made Me

I should never have allowed
myself to love you,
you made me weak
where I was strong;
you made me petals
where I was thorns;
you made me broken
where I was whole.

If there was a way
for me to have known,
maybe I would not have
loved you.

Chloe Harvey

The Sunshine Is Out

The sunshine is out
Should I sing and shout
No, stay indoors
And do some praying

I prayed about
Buying some shampoo
At the Tesco shop
The usual brand will do

I sat in the bedroom
And listened to the computer
Humming
I saw seagulls out the window
It must be Swalwell
My home place in the North East

We have lived here
For a while
The kids have grown up
I've got time on my hands
What shall I do today

The sunshine is out
And time is ticking by
Shall I go to the art club
And paint a lovely picture
Or stay indoors
And dream about when I
Went to Cyprus for my
Daughter's wedding.

Kenneth Mood

February Snow

The Awakening Of Spring.

February snow so light fell sporadically against a sky of aquamarine.
A sparrow pirouetted a distant aerial, its frosty antennae glistening in the bright sun.
Overhead, seagulls flew out of sight over rooftops so near.
Pinioned perfection in flight, whilst carrying a cargo of plumage to bear.
Cumulous clouds then appeared from over a cuneiformed horizon of granite skyline.
A sight to behold as the sun rose on this frosty morn!
The birth of a new day, with the promise of spring carried in chilled air.
Snowdrops now growing where absence had been.
Nature's alarm now alerting their growth as a 'new' year rolls by.
New buds now forming on branches captured the eye.
All this and more gave banquet of hope, and a reasoned goodbye
To a garden of growth, and a sweet lullaby!

Christine Flowers

How Do You Ever Say Goodbye?

Our two souls needed love.
We were brought together by the love above.
I loved you so but you were bad.
You made me cry and very, very sad.
I went and left but you brought me back.
We were two unhappy souls who could not be.
But then one sad day you went away.
I was alone, so alone, I needed you but you were gone.
Is it my fault that I have lost you so,
Was there more I could have done?
So walk beside me every day.
Some day soon I know I must say goodbye.
One day soon this has to be, but until that time
With me you are heart, body and soul.
But soon I know,
I must let you go,
Sleep well my love.
Now you are with the stars above,
I know you are still with me.
Watching me with all your undying
Love.

L Edwards

A Visit To A Purple Bluebell Wood

At Pamphill Wood you have time
To take a steady stroll
You will see a magic carpet
Of lovely bluebells greatly on show,
Sitting around under the brown trees
The sun comes brightly through,
With red dainty toadstools and violets
Scattered all around here and over there,
In the fresh morning dew.

The village's ancient church is asleep,
With a lot of local history for review,
And to look down at the enclosure
A row of trees high up on the road.
On the cricket field, the grass cutter
Is releasing its final winter load.
Behind the trees, a hidden vine somewhere,
Many of Dorset's spooky old tales are told.

Sammy Michael Davis

Sergeant Blackman's Lament

Remember me, from you, taken away.
Locked in cruel fate's grasping claws of steel.
From your caress I can no longer feel –
To sorrow the dark hour, the wasted day.
If time unpicked; I'd walk that loathsome way;
Suffer each good friend's loss, that none could heal.
Change that moment's madness, beyond appeal.
Blank the grim trade that cast the gruesome play.

What alchemy's mix turned off reason's light.
For my next thought, I, or no man could tell.
Making one moment have no wrong or right
Would measured logic deliver this hell.
Stripped of everything I hold so dear!
Remember me, you, who knows this heart well.

Ian Scott

Sleep

Isn't it strange, from the moment we're born
how we need sleep.
Some of us merely sleeping light
while others far more deep.

Eight hours is the ideal
you'll hear the doctors say.
Don't try to fight it
just relax and drift away.

It really is a mystery
how we have a dream.
Pleasurably or in pain
though not always what it may seem.

Some sleep with eyes shut tight
and others open slightly
but far away from the world
trying not to sleep lightly.

No one likes to be woken
so suddenly their heart missed a beat
and most of all we prefer
not to sleep in the cold or heat.

Never take sleep for granted
no matter where you are.
Some sleep in the strangest places
on a beach, in a train or car.

Some enjoy the greatest fantasies
in the Land of Nod.
Winning the lottery, or just having fun
and maybe dreaming of God.

So be sure to get enough shut-eye
wherever you lay down your head.
Sleep is just a part of life
as important as being fed.

Andrew Evzona

Colours

The beautiful bride on her honeymoon swims in the azure blue sea,
Two elegant ladies dine on pink fondant fancies for afternoon tea.
The society hostess looks dazzling in her emerald choker so green,
An effervescent Duchess of Cambridge looks chic in purple and ever so serene.
Two gentlemen sip Italian coffee under the blazing, yellow Tuscany sun,
The toddler in her white sundress frolics on the beach having fun.
A glorious orange sunset breaks out over London town,
A dancer does the tango until dawn in her stunning black gown.
The silvery grey sky beckons the old man to retire early to bed.
The adorable baby takes her afternoon nap with cream-coloured pillows around her weary
head.

Fine Buliciri

In Love's Shadow

In love's shadow
Of that which day provides,
The simplicity of my life.
A shelter over my head,
A settling of my mind.
That yet beyond all this mundane,
As days go by and by.
The nights I could gladly spend,
These the contours of my mind.
A beam I see,
A permanent kiss that stays.
That seat a dream broken, expressed.
For you are always upon my mind.
For all concern that love should stray,
I favour in this deny.
For you are forever the most consistent,
Strong, enamoured.
Forever in my heart of all my eternal days.

Natasha Georgina Georgina Barrell

The Ice Queen

You sit high and mighty in your ivory tower,
You think you have the ultimate power.
To judge, to comment and make me sad.
All I want is, 'It ain't that bad.'
And would it hurt to understand
That I possibly need a helping hand.
An ear to listen to calm my frown,
To lift me up when feelin' down.
But analyse every word I say
And bend round to 'your way'.
You may not realise how hard it is,
To speak to your when I'm in a tiz.
I don't think you'll ever understand
How hard I find it to let you in,
'Cause when I do, my anxieties begin.
So as you sit in your ivory tower,
Knowing things have gone slightly sour,
I sit and home and whittle and worry.
And for that guess I am sorry.
Most of the time we seem to clash,
But give it time and we'll have another bash.

Maggie Evans

Untitled

Slightly apart, the bottom shines.
Feeling like it invites him in.
Whispers, how it longs for you.
He leans in. As she inhales his breath.
Her lips part wider.
She stares at yours.
Biting her lips that are painted deep red.
Tilts her head back, exposing her neck
And that is when he leans in,
Softly kissing her neck, making his way up
To the lips he has been looking for.
They call her the deadliest of sins,
But he says everything worth living for
Kills you one way or another.

Alex Nevin

There By The Tide

Now summer's over
tell me where will you go
now those leaves they
start to fall
and the cold winds
they blow.

Now summer's over
tell me where will you go
I'll go to those places
where old lovers go
to be there again
by her side
there where all of the years
are washed away
there by the tide.

Now summer's over
tell me where will you go
now those leaves
they start to fall
and the cold
winds they blow.

Now summer's over
tell me where
will you go
I'll go to those places
where old lovers go
to be there again
by her side
there where all of the years
are washed away
there by the tide.

K Lake

Success

Pressure, pressure exams.
Pressure, pressure exams.
Family honour, family dishonour.
Burden on my shoulders.
Headaches, migraines, more Red Bull.
Competition from cousins.

Suddenly my mind goes calm.
All I see is paradise.
Shimmering sea like blue diamonds rolling together.
Sand so silky and delicate, like myself.
Sun electrifying and erasing my negative emotions.
My field of vision all fuzzy and distorted.

My glasses are now seated back between my brown eyes.
I have stepped back into reality.
Where time never waits for you.
You work, until your body surrenders itself.
If you do give up, you lose.

My life now depends on today.
Pressure, pressure, exams.
Pressure, pressure, exams.
Family honour, family dishon– our.
My sweat is trickling down my face like droplets.
The clock is ticking, along with my heartbeat.

Gurpawan Khalsa

Forward Poetry Information

We hope you have enjoyed reading this book - and that
you will continue to enjoy it in the coming years.

If you like reading and writing poetry drop us a line, or give
us a call, and we'll send you a free information pack.

Alternatively if you would like to order further copies of this
book or any of our other titles, then please give us a call
or log onto our website at www.forwardpoetry.co.uk

Forward Poetry Information
Remus House
Coltsfoot Drive
Peterborough
PE2 9BF
(01733) 890099